THE TRIUMPHANT MIND

Success Rituals

ABDUL BASIT QAMAR

In memory of my father,

Khurshid Uz Zaman

Contents

	Preface	*i*
	Acknowledgments	*ii*

Understanding Success

1	*Introduction*	2
2	*Types of Success*	2

The Harmony between Materialistic and Spiritual Success

3	*The Significance of Harmony*	7
4	*Ways to Achieve Harmony*	9

Mindset and Attitude

5	*Role of Mindset and Attitude*	26
6	*Developing a Successful Mindset*	27

Time Management and Productivity

7	*Importance of Time Management and Productivity*	37
8	*Enhancing Time Management and Productivity*	38

Networking and Building Relationships

9	*Role of Networking and Building Relationships*	56
10	*Effective Ways to Build Networks and Relationships*	57

Personal Development

11	*Introduction*	68
12	*Essential Skills for Personality Development*	69
13	*Need for a Charismatic Personality*	79

Leadership and Communication

14	*Significance of Leadership and Communication*	95
15	*Improving Leadership Qualities*	95
16	*Broadening Communication Skills*	101

Decision-making and Problem-solving

17	*The Importance of Decision-making and Problem-solving*	109
18	*Strengthening Decision-making and Problem-solving Skills*	110

Creativity and Innovation

19	*The Power of Creativity and Innovation*	*120*
20	*Improving Creative Skills*	*122*

Financial Management and Planning

21	*Introduction*	*131*
22	*Improving Financial Management Skills*	*133*

Self-discipline and Self-control

23	*Introduction*	*150*
24	*Importance of Self-discipline and Self-control*	*151*

Resilience and Adaptability

25	*Introduction*	*168*
26	*Improving Resilience and Adaptability*	*169*

Emotional Intelligence and Stress Management

27	*Introduction*	*182*
28	*Achieving Emotional Intelligence*	*183*
29	*Improving Stress Management*	*195*

Health and Wellness

30	*Significance of Health and Wellness*	*213*

| 31 | The Role of Health and Wellness | 214 |

Setting and Achieving Goals

32	Importance of Goals	227
33	What Happens After Achieving Goals?	227
34	Strategies for Achieving Goals	228

Preface

In "The Triumphant Mind – Success Rituals," offers a comprehensive roadmap for achieving success in all areas of life. From materialistic success to spiritual fulfillment, this book covers the essential traits and characteristics needed to excel in today's fast-paced world.

With a focus on practical strategies and actionable steps, this book provides readers with the tools they need to start on the path to success. Whether you're looking to improve your productivity, build stronger relationships, or develop your leadership skills, this book has something for everyone.

With chapters on topics such as mindset, attitude, time management, networking, and financial management, this book is an invaluable resource for anyone looking to take control of their life and achieve their goals. Written by an experienced professional with a deep understanding of what it takes to succeed, "The Triumphant Mind – Success Rituals" is a must-read for anyone looking to reach the next level of success.

This book is for anyone who is looking to take their life to the next level and wants to learn the secrets of success. It is written by Abdul Basit Qamar aka Abdul B. Qamar, who has shared his experience and the insights that have helped him to become successful. It will be a great help for those who want to become successful but don't know how to get started.

Acknowledgments

First and foremost, I would like to express my deepest gratitude to my friends and family for their unwavering support and encouragement throughout the writing process of this book. Their love and support have been invaluable and have made this journey possible.

I would also like to thank *Mahnoor Shahid*, for guiding me with her wisdom and expertise. Her motivational words and support have been instrumental in shaping the content of this book.

I would also like to thank the team at Kindle Direct Publishing (KDP), Amazon, for their hard work and dedication in bringing this book to life. Their expertise and professionalism have been essential in bringing this project to fruition.

Finally, I would like to express my appreciation to all of my readers. Your support and encouragement have been the driving force behind this book and I hope that it will be of value to you in your journey toward success.

Once again, thank you to everyone who has supported me throughout this process. I am deeply grateful for your contributions and support.

Understanding Success

Overview

- ❖ *Introduction*
- ❖ *Types of Success*
    - ✓ *Materialistic Success*
    - ✓ *Spiritual Success*

INTRODUCTION

Success has many definitions, as its meaning is different for everyone. The concept of success can vary depending on the individual and the context, as it can pertain to personal, professional, or societal aspirations. Success can be measured in many ways such as financial wealth, fame, power, happiness, or personal fulfillment. However, as a whole, it can be defined as the accomplishment of an aim or purpose. It can also be seen as achieving a desired outcome or level of achievement.

TYPES OF SUCCESS

Typically, success can be of two types: materialistic or spiritual – Let's see what these two mean…

1. Materialistic Success

Materialistic success refers to achieving success through the acquisition of material possessions, such as money, property, and luxury goods. It is often associated with the idea that having more wealth, status symbols, and material possessions will lead to happiness and fulfillment. Materialistic success is often measured by one's financial wealth, the number and value of possessions they have, and the status one holds in society. It is often seen as a way of measuring one's worth and status in society, by comparing the possessions they have to those of others. An example of materialistic success would be an individual who works tirelessly to attain a high-paying job, or to build a successful business, with the ultimate goal of accumulating wealth and acquiring material possessions such as a luxury car, a large house, and designer clothing.

This person may find a sense of satisfaction and fulfillment in being able to afford the finer things in life, and in being able to show off their wealth and status to others. This individual may define success as being able to buy whatever they want and to live a lavish lifestyle. They may be constantly seeking to acquire new possessions and improve their financial status. However, it's important to note that materialistic success is not universally accepted as a true measure of success.

2. Spiritual Success

Some people may argue that true success should be measured by the quality of one's relationships, the impact one has on others, and their overall level of happiness and fulfillment, rather than just by their material possessions. This type of success is called a spiritual one. But wait, why not dig it more… Well, Spiritual success refers to achieving a sense of inner peace, fulfillment, and harmony through the cultivation of one's spiritual or inner self. It can be seen as a way of measuring success that goes beyond material possessions and external markers of achievement. For some individuals, spiritual success may mean finding a deeper sense of purpose and meaning in their lives and connecting with a higher power or universal consciousness. This may involve practices such as meditation, prayer, and self-reflection. An example of spiritual success might be an individual who has struggled with addiction, but through spiritual practices such as meditation and mindfulness, they can find peace and contentment within themselves and can overcome their addiction without relying on external validation or material possessions. They may find success in being able to live a fulfilling life and be at peace with themselves.

Now, *stop for a moment and think* – on which type of success one should focus? Materialistic success? Okay, then it should be the spiritual one, no? Or you're not sure about it? Alright, let me continue….

See, it's worth noting that while material and spiritual success are often seen as separate and distinct, it is possible to strive for both and find a balance and harmony between them. Real wisdom is to think and strive for both.

One (materialistic success) should be treated as a physical need for enduring in this world, whereas the other one (spiritual success) should be considered a vital mental state for the well-being of the mind or soul.

Time to ponder again – How to become successful by achieving both, materialistic and spiritual success together? Well, one can strive for both material and spiritual success by finding a balance between the two. This may involve setting both material and spiritual goals and working towards achieving them in a holistic and balanced way.

For example, an individual may set a goal to attain a high-paying job or to build a successful business, but also make a conscious effort to cultivate their inner self through spiritual practices such as meditation, prayer, or self-reflection. This person may also make a point to use their material success to help others and make a positive impact in the world. They could give back to the community, volunteer, or donate to charity.

Another way to achieve balance is to ensure that material success is not the ultimate goal, but rather a means to an end. This means that the ultimate goal is not to accumulate wealth and possessions, but rather to use them to achieve inner peace, fulfillment, and happiness.

It's also important to evaluate one's priorities and values and to make sure that they align with both material and spiritual goals. This may involve re-evaluating what success means to an individual, and making sure that material success is not the only measure of worth and fulfillment.

Ultimately, achieving a balance between material and spiritual success will look different for each person, and individuals need to find a way that works best for them. You must be thinking how can you start with it, no? Don't worry, continue reading! Soon, in the next chapter, you are going to discover some strategies to achieve a balance between materialistic and spiritual success.

The Harmony between Materialistic and Spiritual Success

Overview

- ❖ *The Significance of Harmony*
- ❖ *Ways to Achieve Harmony*
    - ✓ *Mindfulness and Meditation*
    - ✓ *Gratitude and Appreciation*
    - ✓ *Setting Intentions*
    - ✓ *Time Management*
    - ✓ *Finding Purpose*
    - ✓ *Building Supportive Relationships*
    - ✓ *Helping Others*
    - ✓ *Self-reflection*
    - ✓ *Simplicity*
    - ✓ *Self-efficiency*
    - ✓ *Practicing Self-compassion*
    - ✓ *Finding a Balance between Action and Rest*
    - ✓ *Cultivating Inner Peace*
    - ✓ *Giving Back*
    - ✓ *Letting Go of your Ego*

THE SIGNIFICANCE OF HARMONY

Developing a balance or harmony between materialistic and spiritual success is significant because it allows individuals to achieve a sense of fulfillment and well-being in both their personal and professional lives. Materialistic success often refers to achieving financial wealth and status, while spiritual success typically refers to achieving inner peace, contentment, and a sense of purpose.

When individuals focus solely on materialistic success, they may find that they are not satisfied or fulfilled, even if they have achieved a high level of financial and professional success. On the other hand, when individuals focus only on spiritual success, they may lack the resources and opportunities necessary to achieve their goals and fulfill their needs.

When individuals find a balance between materialistic and spiritual success, they can find meaning and purpose in their lives and can live their lives with a sense of inner peace and contentment. This balance allows them to have the necessary resources to achieve their goals while not losing sight of their inner self and values.

Additionally, balancing materialistic and spiritual success can help individuals to have a better perspective in life, have a better relationship with people, and to be more compassionate and understanding. It can also help them to make better decisions, to have a better work-life balance, and to be more resilient.

In summary, developing harmony between materialistic

and spiritual success is significant because it allows individuals to achieve a sense of fulfillment and well-being in all aspects of their lives, and to live with a sense of inner peace and contentment.

For Example:

- A highly successful business executive has achieved a high level of financial success but feels unfulfilled and empty. By developing harmony between materialistic and spiritual success, the executive starts to focus on inner growth and self-discovery, which leads to a greater sense of purpose and meaning in their life. They start to volunteer in their community and make time for activities such as meditation and yoga, which helps them to feel more content and fulfilled.

- A young professional who is ambitious and driven to succeed, but often finds themselves feeling stressed, anxious, and disconnected from their inner self. By developing harmony between materialistic and spiritual success, this individual learns to prioritize self-care, and make time for activities such as journaling, mindfulness, and connecting with nature.

    This helps them to find a sense of inner peace and contentment, which allows them to be more productive, creative, and focused in their professional life. They also learn to be more compassionate and understanding toward others, which helps them to build better relationships and to be a better leader.

WAYS TO ACHIEVE HARMONY

Achieving harmony between materialistic and spiritual success can be a challenging task, but it can be done by following some practices. Here are some ways to achieve harmony between materialistic and spiritual success:

1. Mindfulness and Meditation

Mindfulness and meditation can help in developing harmony between materialistic and spiritual success by promoting a balanced and non-judgmental perspective toward one's goals and aspirations. These practices can help one to become more aware of the present moment, which can lead to a greater sense of contentment and fulfillment, regardless of one's material success. Additionally, they can also help one to become more attuned to one's inner values and priorities, which can lead to a greater alignment between one's actions and one's deeper sense of purpose. This can ultimately lead to a sense of harmony between one's material and spiritual success.

For example, an individual who is focused on achieving financial success may find that through practicing mindfulness and meditation, they begin to realize that money is not the only important thing in life. They may begin to prioritize their time with family and friends and appreciate the value of non-material things like nature and art. As a result, they may find that they can achieve a greater sense of balance in their lives and that they can enjoy their material success in a more meaningful way.

2. *Gratitude and Appreciation*

Gratitude and appreciation can help in developing harmony between materialistic and spiritual success by promoting a positive and thankful attitude toward one's life and circumstances. These practices can help one to focus on the present moment and appreciate what one already has, rather than constantly striving for more. This can lead to a greater sense of contentment and fulfillment, regardless of one's material success. Additionally, gratitude and appreciation can also help one to become more attuned to the interconnectedness of all things, which can foster a sense of interconnectedness and community. This can ultimately lead to a sense of harmony between one's material and spiritual success.

Practicing gratitude and appreciation can also shift one's focus to the present moment and the good things that one already has, instead of always focusing on what one lacks. It can lead to a greater sense of contentment and satisfaction with one's life, which can help to reduce stress and anxiety. It can also foster a more optimistic outlook on life, which can have a positive impact on one's overall well-being and happiness. For example, an individual may have a goal of achieving financial success and owning a large house, but through the practice of gratitude and appreciation, they may come to realize that the true source of happiness and fulfillment is found in the relationships they have with loved ones, and the experiences they share with them. Instead of constantly striving for more wealth and possessions, they may come to appreciate and value the simple pleasures in life such as spending time with family or enjoying nature. This shift in perspective can lead to a greater sense of contentment and fulfillment, regardless of their material success.

Additionally, regularly practicing gratitude and appreciation can also foster a sense of interconnectedness and community, which can ultimately lead to a sense of harmony between one's material and spiritual success. It can also help one to become more attuned to one's inner values and priorities, and align one's actions with one's deeper sense of purpose.

3. Setting Intentions

Setting intentions can help to develop a balance between material and spiritual success by providing a clear direction and purpose for one's actions. By setting intentions, individuals can align their actions with their values and goals, which can lead to a greater sense of meaning and fulfillment in their lives. Additionally, setting intentions can also help to promote a sense of focus and discipline, which can be beneficial for achieving both material and spiritual success.

For example, an individual who is focused on achieving

financial success may set the intention to increase their income by a certain amount within a specific timeframe. At the same time, they may also set the intention to spend more quality time with family and friends and to volunteer for a cause that they are passionate about. By setting these intentions, the individual can align their actions with their values and priorities and can work towards achieving a balance between material and spiritual success. As a result, they may find that they can achieve their financial goals while also feeling more fulfilled and content in their personal life.

4. *Time Management*

Time management can help to develop a balance between material and spiritual success by allowing individuals to prioritize their time and make the most of the opportunities that they have. By effectively managing their time, individuals can ensure that they are spending their time in ways that align with their values and goals, which can lead to a greater sense of purpose and fulfillment. Additionally, time management can also help to reduce stress and increase productivity, which can be beneficial for achieving both material and spiritual success.

For example, an individual who is focused on achieving financial success may use time management techniques to prioritize their work and make the most of their time.

They may also set aside time for personal pursuits such as spending time with family and friends, practicing mindfulness and meditation, or volunteering for a cause they are passionate about. By effectively managing their time, they can balance their material and spiritual pursuits, and increase their chances of achieving both. As a result, they may find that they not only reach their financial goals but also feel more fulfilled and content in their personal life.

5. *Finding Purpose*

Finding purpose can help to develop a balance between material and spiritual success by providing a sense of meaning and direction for one's actions. When individuals have a clear sense of purpose, they are more likely to align their actions with their values and goals, which can lead to a greater sense of fulfillment and satisfaction. Additionally, having a sense of purpose can also help to promote a sense of motivation and drive, which can be beneficial for achieving both material and spiritual success.

For example, an individual who is focused on achieving financial success may find that by identifying their purpose and the reason behind their actions, they become more motivated to work harder and achieve their goals. At the same time, they may also find that having a clear purpose for their actions helps them to prioritize their time, and ensure that they are also taking time for things that are important for their personal growth and wellbeing such as spending time with family and friends, practicing mindfulness and meditation or volunteer for a cause they are passionate about. By having a clear sense of purpose, they can balance their material and spiritual pursuits, and increase their chances of achieving both. They may find that they not only reach their financial goals but also feel more fulfilled and content in their personal life.

6. *Building Supportive Relationships*

Building supportive relationships can help to develop a balance between material and spiritual success by providing a sense of connection and community, which can be essential for personal growth and well-being. Having supportive relationships can also provide valuable support and guidance, which can be beneficial for achieving both material and spiritual success. When individuals have a supportive network of people around them, they are more likely to feel valued, understood, and motivated to pursue their goals.

For example, an individual who is focused on achieving financial success may find that by building supportive relationships with colleagues, mentors, and friends, they can achieve their goals more efficiently. They may also find that having a supportive network of people in their life helps to provide a sense of balance and perspective, which can be essential for achieving a sense of harmony between material and spiritual success. They may be more likely to take time to reflect on their actions and prioritize the things that are important to them, such as spending time with family and friends, practicing mindfulness and meditation, or volunteering for a cause they are passionate about. By having a supportive network of people, they can balance their material and spiritual pursuits, and increase their chances of achieving both. They may find that they not only reach their financial goals but also feel more fulfilled and content in their personal life.

7. Helping Others

Helping others can help to develop a balance between material and spiritual success by promoting a sense of connection and purpose, and by providing a sense of fulfillment that can be difficult to achieve through material success alone. When individuals engage in acts of kindness and generosity, they can experience a sense of joy and fulfillment that is not dependent on material possessions. Helping others can also promote a sense of gratitude and perspective, which can be beneficial for achieving both material and spiritual success.

For example, an individual who is focused on achieving financial success may find that by volunteering for a cause they are passionate about, they can gain a sense of purpose and fulfillment that is not dependent on their financial success. They may also find that by helping others, they can gain a deeper appreciation for their blessings and opportunities, which can help to promote a sense of contentment and gratitude. By helping others, they can balance their material and spiritual pursuits, and increase their chances of achieving both. They may find that they not only reach their financial goals but also feel more fulfilled and content in their personal life.

8. *Self-reflection*

Self-reflection can help to develop a balance between material and spiritual success by promoting greater awareness of one's thoughts, emotions, and actions. By regularly reflecting on one's experiences, individuals can gain a greater understanding of their values and priorities, which can lead to a greater alignment between their actions and their personal goals.

This can also lead to greater insight into one's motivations and the meaning behind their actions, which can help to promote a sense of balance and harmony between material and spiritual success. For example, an individual who is focused on achieving financial success may find that through regular self-reflection, they begin to realize that money is not the only important thing in life.

They may begin to question their motivations and priorities and may come to realize that they also want to prioritize their time with family and friends and appreciate the value of non-material things like nature and art. As a result, they may find that they can achieve a greater sense of balance and harmony in their lives and that they can enjoy their material success in a more meaningful way. Self-reflection can also help them to identify areas of their life that may need adjustments and to make changes that align with their values and goals.

9. Simplicity

Simplicity can help to develop a balance between material and spiritual success by promoting a sense of contentment and fulfillment that is not dependent on material possessions. By simplifying one's life, individuals can reduce stress and distractions, and can focus on what is truly important to them. This can also help to promote a greater sense of gratitude and appreciation for the things that one already has, which can lead to a greater sense of contentment and fulfillment.

For example, an individual who is focused on achieving financial success may find that by simplifying their life, they can achieve a greater sense of balance and harmony in their lives. They may choose to downsize their home, sell their car and other possessions, and focus on the things that truly matter to them such as their relationships and personal growth. They may find that by simplifying their life, they can reduce stress and distractions, and can focus on what is truly important to them.

As a result, they may find that they can achieve a greater sense of balance and harmony in their lives and that they can enjoy their material success in a more meaningful way. They may also find that they are more content with what they have and less focused on constantly acquiring more possessions, which can help to create a more harmonious balance between material and spiritual success.

10. Self-efficiency

Self-efficiency can help to develop a balance between material and spiritual success by promoting a sense of control and agency over one's life. When individuals are self-efficient, they are more likely to set clear goals and take action toward achieving them. They also tend to be more organized and productive, which can be beneficial for achieving both material and spiritual success. Additionally, being self-efficient can also help individuals to manage their time and energy more effectively, which can be crucial for achieving a sense of balance and harmony between material and spiritual pursuits.

For example, an individual who is focused on achieving financial success may find that by developing their self-efficiency, they are better able to set clear goals and take action towards achieving them. They may also find that by being more organized and productive, they can manage their time and energy more effectively, which allows them to prioritize the things that are important to them, such as spending time with family and friends, practicing mindfulness and meditation, or volunteering for a cause they are passionate about.

By becoming more self-efficient, they can balance their material and spiritual pursuits, and increase their chances of achieving both. They may find that they not only reach their financial goals but also feel more fulfilled and content in their personal life.

11. Practicing Self-compassion

Practicing self-compassion can help to develop a balance between material and spiritual success by promoting a greater sense of self-acceptance and understanding, which can lead to a greater sense of contentment and fulfillment. When individuals practice self-compassion, they are more likely to be kind and understanding towards themselves, even when they make mistakes or fall short of their goals. This can help to promote a greater sense of resilience and perseverance, which can be beneficial for achieving both material and spiritual success. Additionally, practicing self-compassion can also help individuals to view their failures and mistakes as opportunities for growth and learning, which can be crucial for achieving a sense of balance and harmony between material and spiritual pursuits.

For example, an individual who is focused on achieving financial success may find that by practicing self-compassion, they can view their failures and mistakes as opportunities for growth and learning. They may also find that by being kind and understanding towards themselves, they can persevere and achieve their goals even in the face of challenges. They may also find that by practicing self-compassion, they can focus on the present moment, and appreciate the things that are important to them, such as spending time with family and friends, practicing mindfulness and meditation, or volunteering for a cause they are passionate about. By practicing self-compassion, they can balance their material and spiritual pursuits, and increase their chances of achieving both. They may find that they not only reach their financial goals but also feel more fulfilled and content in their personal life.

12. Finding a Balance between Action and Rest

Finding a balance between action and rest can help to develop a harmony between material and spiritual success by promoting physical and mental well-being, which can be crucial for achieving both material and spiritual goals. When individuals find a balance between action and rest, they are more likely to have the energy and focus needed to take action toward achieving their goals. They also tend to be more resilient, better able to manage stress and have a better sense of overall well-being. Additionally, finding a balance between action and rest can also help individuals to prioritize their time and energy, which can be crucial for achieving a sense of balance and harmony between material and spiritual pursuits.

For example, an individual who is focused on achieving financial success may find that by finding a balance between action and rest, they can better manage stress and have more energy to pursue their goals. They may also find that by taking regular breaks and engaging in activities that promote rest, such as exercise, meditation, or spending time with friends and family, they are better able to focus and be productive when working on achieving their financial goals. They may also find that by finding a balance between action and rest, they can prioritize their time and energy, and ensure that they are also taking time for things that are important for their personal growth and well-being. By finding a balance between action and rest, they can balance their material and spiritual pursuits, and increase their chances of achieving both. They may find that they not only reach their financial goals but also feel more fulfilled and content in their personal life.

13. Cultivating Inner Peace

Cultivating inner peace can help to develop a harmony between material and spiritual success by promoting a sense of contentment and fulfillment that is not dependent on material possessions or external circumstances. Inner peace can be cultivated through practices such as mindfulness, meditation, and self-reflection, which can help individuals to detach from their thoughts and emotions, and focus on the present moment. When individuals can cultivate inner peace, they are more likely to experience a sense of contentment and fulfillment, even in the face of challenges or setbacks. Additionally, cultivating inner peace can also help individuals to view their experiences and circumstances with a sense of perspective, which can be beneficial for achieving both material and spiritual success.

For example, an individual who is focused on achieving financial success may find that by cultivating inner peace, they can detach from their thoughts and emotions, and focus on the present moment. They may also find that by cultivating inner peace, they can view their experiences and circumstances with a sense of perspective, which allows them to appreciate the things that are truly important to them, such as their relationships and personal growth. By cultivating inner peace, they can balance their material and spiritual pursuits, and increase their chances of achieving both. They may find that they not only reach their financial goals but also feel more fulfilled and content in their personal life. They may also find that they are less affected by external events and more centered on what truly matters to them.

14. Giving Back

Giving back can help to develop a harmony between material and spiritual success by promoting a sense of connection and purpose, and by providing a sense of fulfillment that can be difficult to achieve through material success alone. When individuals engage in acts of kindness and generosity towards others, they can experience a sense of joy and fulfillment that is not dependent on material possessions. Giving back can also promote a sense of gratitude and perspective, which can be beneficial for achieving both material and spiritual success. Additionally, it can also help to reduce the negative effects of materialism by fostering a sense of purpose, community, and connection.

For example, an individual who is focused on achieving financial success may find that by giving back to their community through volunteering, mentoring, or donating to a cause they care about, they can gain a sense of purpose and fulfillment that is not dependent on their financial success. They may also find that by giving back, they can gain a deeper appreciation for their blessings and opportunities, which can help to promote a sense of contentment and gratitude. By giving back, they can balance their material and spiritual pursuits, and increase their chances of achieving both. They may find that they not only reach their financial goals but also feel more fulfilled and content in their personal life. They may also find that they are more connected to the community and more motivated to make a positive impact on the world.

15. Letting Go of your Ego

Letting go of one's ego can help to develop a harmony between material and spiritual success by promoting a greater sense of humility and perspective. When individuals let go of their egos, they are more likely to focus on the needs of others and to be more open to learning and growth. This can lead to a greater sense of connection and fulfillment, which can be beneficial for achieving both material and spiritual success. Additionally, letting go of one's ego can also help individuals to detach from their thoughts and emotions, and focus on the present moment which can help to cultivate inner peace.

For example, an individual who is focused on achieving financial success may find that by letting go of their ego, they can detach from their thoughts and emotions, and focus on the present moment. They may also find that by letting go of their ego, they can focus on the needs of others and be more open to learning and growth. This can lead to a greater sense of connection and fulfillment, which can be beneficial for achieving both material and spiritual success. They may also find that by letting go of their ego they can be more humble, and more willing to collaborate, share and listen to others which can help them to achieve their goals more efficiently. By letting go of their ego, they can balance their material and spiritual pursuits, and increase their chances of achieving both. They may find that they not only reach their financial goals but also feel more fulfilled and content in their personal life.

Mindset and Attitude

Overview

- ❖ *Role of Mindset and Attitude*
- ❖ *Developing a Successful Mindset*
  - ✓ *Positive Mindset*
  - ✓ *Growth Mindset*
  - ✓ *The Impact of Negative Thinking*
  - ✓ *The Link between Mindset and Self-Belief*
  - ✓ *Winning Attitude*
  - ✓ *The Impact of Resilience and Grit*
  - ✓ *Role of Mindfulness*
  - ✓ *Developing a Positive Attitude in the Workplace*
  - ✓ *The Connection between Attitude and Leadership*
  - ✓ *Attitude for Building Relationships*

ROLE OF MINDSET AND ATTITUDE

Mindset and attitude play a crucial role in achieving success. A positive mindset and attitude can help individuals to stay motivated, overcome obstacles, and maintain a sense of perspective when faced with challenges. A negative mindset and attitude, on the other hand, can lead to feelings of discouragement and helplessness, which can make it more difficult to achieve success.

One example of the role of mindset and attitude in achieving success is in the area of personal and professional development. An individual with a growth mindset will approach challenges as opportunities for learning and growth, while someone with a fixed mindset may see challenges as personal failures. A person with a growth mindset will be more likely to persevere and achieve their goals, while a person with a fixed mindset may give up more easily.

Another example of the role of mindset and attitude in achieving success is in the area of relationships. An individual with a positive attitude towards relationships will approach them with an open mind and will be more likely to build strong and lasting connections with others. On the other hand, an individual with a negative attitude towards relationships may struggle to form meaningful connections and may find it harder to achieve success in their personal and professional life. In both examples, it's clear that a positive mindset and attitude can help individuals to achieve success in various areas of their lives, while a negative mindset and attitude can make in more difficult to achieve success.

DEVELOPING A SUCCESSFUL MINDSET

Developing a successful mindset involves cultivating a set of attitudes and beliefs that can help you to achieve your goals and reach your full potential. Here are some key elements of a successful mindset:

1. Positive Mindset

A positive mindset can help in developing a successful mindset by fostering a belief in oneself and one's abilities, as well as a willingness to take on challenges and persevere through difficulties.

An example of this might be an individual who approaches a difficult task with a positive attitude, believing in their ability to complete it successfully and putting in the necessary effort and time to achieve their goal, despite any obstacles that may arise. This person would be more likely to succeed than someone with a defeatist mindset.

2. Growth Mindset

A growth mindset can help in developing a successful mindset by emphasizing the belief that one's abilities and intelligence can be developed and improved through effort and learning. This mindset encourages individuals to take on challenges and to learn from failures or mistakes, rather than being discouraged by them. An example of this might be an individual who is not particularly skilled at a certain task, but with a growth mindset, they approach the task with a willingness to learn, and persistence. They don't shy away from challenges but instead embrace them as opportunities for growth and development, and as a result, they become skilled and successful in that task.

3. The Impact of Negative Thinking

The impact of negative thinking can hinder the development of a successful mindset by leading to feelings of self-doubt, low self-esteem, and a lack of motivation. Negative thoughts can also cause individuals to avoid taking on challenges or to give up easily when faced with difficulties.

An example of this might be an individual who is constantly telling themselves they can't do anything, they give up easily, and they avoid taking on new challenges. This person would be less likely to succeed than someone who has a more optimistic mindset. By recognizing and changing negative thought patterns, an individual can develop a more successful mindset and increase their chances of achieving their goals.

It's important to note that it's normal to have negative thoughts and emotions, but when it becomes too overwhelming and starts affecting your daily life, it's important to seek help from a professional.

HOW TO OVERCOME NEGATIVE THINKING?

There are several ways to overcome negative thoughts. Some of them include:

a) Recognize Negative thoughts

The first step in overcoming negative thoughts is to recognize when they occur. By becoming aware of your negative thoughts, you can begin to challenge and change them.

b) Challenge Negative thoughts

Once you've identified your negative thoughts, you can start to challenge them. Ask yourself if the thought is based on fact or if it's just a negative assumption. Is the thought realistic or is it an exaggeration?

c) Replace Negative thoughts with Positive ones

Once you've challenged a negative thought, you can replace it with a more positive one. For example, instead of thinking "I'll never be able to do this," try thinking "I can do this, and I'll keep working on it until I succeed.

d) Practice Mindfulness

Mindfulness can help you to be more aware of your thoughts and emotions, and it can help you to stay in the present moment. This can be a powerful tool for overcoming negative thoughts.

e) Get Support

Sometimes, talking to someone you trust can help you to overcome negative thoughts. Whether it's a friend, a family member, or a therapist, having someone to talk to can provide a different perspective and help you to feel more supported.

f) Seek Professional Help

If negative thoughts are overwhelming and affecting your daily life, it's important to seek help from a professional like a therapist or counselor. They can help you to identify the source of your negative thoughts and provide strategies to overcome them.

It's important to keep in mind that negative thoughts are a normal part of the human experience, but when they become overwhelming and start affecting your daily life, it's important to take action to overcome them.

4. The Link between Mindset and Self-Belief

The link between mindset and self-belief can play a key role in developing a successful mindset. A person's mindset shapes their beliefs about themselves and their abilities, and these beliefs in turn influence their actions and decisions. A person with a positive mindset and strong self-belief is more likely to take on challenges, persevere through difficulties, and ultimately achieve their goals.

An example of this might be an individual who has a strong belief in their abilities, they are confident in their decision-making, and are not afraid to take on new challenges. They see failures as learning opportunities and they don't let them discourage them. This person would be more likely to succeed than someone who lacks self-belief and has a negative mindset. By working on building self-belief and adopting a positive mindset, an individual can increase their chances of success in their personal and professional life.

5. *Winning Attitude*

A winning attitude can help in developing a successful mindset by fostering a sense of determination, optimism, and resilience. A person with a winning attitude is more likely to take on challenges, set and work towards goals, and persevere through difficulties. They also tend to be more resilient in the face of setbacks and more likely to bounce back from failures.

An example of this might be an individual who has a clear vision of what they want to achieve, and they are willing to put in the work to make it happen. They have a "can do" attitude, they are not afraid of taking risks and they don't let setbacks discourage them. They take responsibility for their actions, and they don't blame external factors for their failures. This person would be more likely to succeed than someone who lacks motivation and has a negative mindset. By developing a winning attitude, an individual can increase their chances of success in their personal and professional life.

6. The Impact of Resilience and Grit

Resilience and grit can play a key role in developing a successful mindset by helping individuals to bounce back from setbacks and to persevere through difficult times. Resilience is the ability to adapt and cope with adversity, while grit is a combination of passion and perseverance for long-term goals.

An example of this might be an individual who is working towards a long-term goal, they have setbacks and failures along the way, but they don't let that discourage them. They have the grit to stick with it and the resilience to adapt to the changes and keep moving forward.

This person would be more likely to achieve their goal than someone who gives up easily and lacks resilience and grit. By developing resilience and grit, an individual can increase their chances of success in their personal and professional life.

It's important to note that resilience and grit are not only about bouncing back from failures and setbacks, but also about the ability to bounce forward, to learn from those experiences, and to use them to become stronger, more flexible, and more capable.

7. Role of Mindfulness

Mindfulness can help in developing a successful mindset by allowing individuals to be present in the moment, focus their attention, and be aware of their thoughts and emotions. Practicing mindfulness can help to reduce stress and anxiety and increase self-awareness. It can also help individuals to stay calm and focused in the face of challenges and be more resilient in the face of setbacks.

An example of this might be an individual who is working towards a long-term goal but has a lot of stress and anxiety about it. By practicing mindfulness, these people become more aware of their thoughts and emotions, and they learn to manage their stress and anxiety better. They can focus on the task at hand and stay calm in the face of challenges. As a result, they are more likely to achieve their goal than someone who is constantly worried and anxious. By incorporating mindfulness into their daily routine, an individual can improve their ability to focus, stay calm, and achieve their goals.

8. Developing a Positive Attitude in the Workplace

Developing a positive attitude in the workplace can help in developing a successful mindset by fostering a supportive and productive work environment. A positive attitude can lead to increased motivation, improved communication, and better problem-solving skills. It can also lead to increased job satisfaction and better relationships with colleagues. An example of this might be an individual who is a team leader, they have a positive attitude, are supportive and they create a positive and productive work environment. They encourage open communication and appreciate their team member's efforts and they are willing to help when needed. As a result, their team members are more motivated, productive, and engaged in their work. This team leader would be more likely to achieve their goals than someone negative and creates a toxic work environment. By developing a positive attitude and fostering a positive work environment, an individual can increase their chances of success and the success of the team and the company.

9. The Connection between Attitude and Leadership

The connection between attitude and leadership can play a key role in developing a successful mindset. A leader's attitude sets the tone for the entire team and can have a significant impact on team morale, motivation, and productivity. A leader with a positive attitude is more likely to inspire and motivate their team, which can lead to better performance and improved results.

An example of this might be a leader who is facing a difficult situation, but instead of getting discouraged, they maintain a positive attitude, they communicate with their team effectively, they look for solutions, and they remain confident in the team's ability to overcome the challenge. This leader's positivity and confidence would be contagious and would help their team to stay motivated, focused, and engaged. This leader would be more likely to achieve their goals than someone negative and demotivating. By developing a positive attitude, and connecting it with their leadership skills, an individual can increase their chances of success and the success of their team and organization.

10. Attitude for Building Relationships

A positive attitude can play a key role in building relationships. A person with a positive attitude is more likely to be approachable, friendly, and open-minded. They are also more likely to be able to communicate effectively and build trust with others. A positive attitude can also lead to better conflict resolution and problem-solving skills.

An example of this might be an individual who is a sales representative, they have a positive attitude, they are empathetic and they build strong relationships with their clients. They listen to their client's needs and concerns, they are willing to help and they are responsive to their client's requests. As a result, they have a high retention rate of clients and they can close more deals. This sales representative would be more likely to achieve their goals than someone negative and not responsive to their client's needs. By developing a positive attitude and building strong relationships, an individual can increase their chances of success in their personal and professional life.

Time Management and Productivity

Overview

- ❖ *Importance of Time Management and Productivity*
- ❖ *Enhancing Time Management and Productivity*
    - ✓ *Setting Clear Goals and Priorities*
    - ✓ *Creating a Schedule and Sticking to it*
    - ✓ *Eliminating Distractions and Time-wasters*
    - ✓ *Managing Email and Communication Effectively*
    - ✓ *Using Technology to Automate Repetitive Tasks*
    - ✓ *Prioritizing Self-care and Rest*
    - ✓ *Learning to Say "no" to Non-essential Commitments*
    - ✓ *Breaking up Large tasks into Smaller, Manageable Chunks*
    - ✓ *Using Techniques that can boost Focus and Concentration*
    - ✓ *Constantly Reviewing and Adjusting your Time Management Strategies*
    - ✓ *Delegating Tasks to Others*
    - ✓ *Batching similar tasks Together*
    - ✓ *Using a Task manager or Planner*
    - ✓ *Using a Calendar*
    - ✓ *Building good Habits and Routines*

IMPORTANCE OF TIME MANAGEMENT AND PRODUCTIVITY

Time management is the process of planning and organizing how to allocate time effectively and efficiently to accomplish specific tasks, goals, and projects.

Time management and productivity are important for becoming successful because they help individuals to make the most of their time and to achieve their goals.

When people manage their time and use it productively, they can accomplish more in less time, which can lead to greater success in their personal and professional lives.

For example, a business owner who can manage their time effectively and stay productive can complete more tasks, meet more deadlines and increase their revenue.

Another example, is a student who can manage their time effectively and stay productive, can study more effectively, complete assignments and projects on time, and achieve better grades.

Effective time management and productivity require discipline, focus, and a clear understanding of one's goals, but with practice and persistence, it can be developed and leads to greater success.

ENHANCING TIME MANAGEMENT AND PRODUCTIVITY

Here are some effective tips for enhancing time management and productivity:

1. Setting Clear Goals and Priorities

Setting clear goals and priorities can help in time management and productivity by providing a clear focus and direction for one's efforts. When individuals have a clear understanding of what they want to achieve and how they want to achieve it, they are more likely to stay motivated and on track.

For example, a business owner who sets clear and measurable goals for their business, such as increasing revenue by a certain percentage within a specific time frame, and prioritizes the tasks and actions necessary to achieve those goals, is more likely to be more successful than someone who has no clear goals or plan in place. By setting clear goals, the business owner can focus on what is important and avoid wasting time on non-essential tasks.

In the same way, a student who sets clear academic goals, such as getting a certain GPA, and prioritizes their study time and assignments, is more likely to be successful than someone who is not clear on what they want to achieve. By setting goals and prioritizing tasks, the student can stay focused and motivated, and avoid procrastination, which ultimately leads to better performance.

In a nutshell, setting clear goals and priorities can help individuals to stay motivated, focused, and on track, which leads to better time management and productivity.

2. Creating a Schedule and Sticking to it

Creating a schedule and sticking to it can help in time management and productivity by providing structure and organization for one's time. A schedule can help individuals to prioritize tasks, set and meet deadlines, and avoid procrastination.

For example, a professional who creates a daily schedule that includes specific time slots for work tasks, meetings, exercise, and personal time and sticks to it, is more likely to be productive and efficient than someone who has no schedule in place.

By following the schedule, the professional can ensure that they are allocating sufficient time for important tasks and avoiding wasting time on non-essential activities.

Another example is a student who creates a weekly schedule that includes specific time slots for studying, class preparation, and extracurricular activities, and sticks to it is more likely to achieve academic success than someone who has no schedule in place. By following the schedule, the student can ensure that they are allocating sufficient time for studying and preparing for exams and avoid procrastination.

In summary, creating a schedule and sticking to it can help individuals to stay organized, focused, and efficient, which leads to better time management and productivity. It's important to keep in mind that flexibility is also important, and it's necessary to adjust the schedule as needed, but the key is to stick to it as much as possible.

3. Eliminating Distractions and Time-wasters

Eliminating distractions and time-wasters can help in time management and productivity by allowing individuals to focus on important tasks and avoid wasting time on non-essential activities. Distractions and time-wasters can come in many forms, such as social media, email notifications, unnecessary meetings, and procrastination.

By identifying and eliminating these distractions and time-wasters, individuals can increase their productivity and achieve their goals more efficiently.

For example, an office worker who eliminates distractions like social media and email notifications during work hours, and avoids unnecessary meetings, will be able to focus on their work and complete tasks more efficiently than someone who is constantly distracted. This worker would be more productive and would be able to achieve more in less time.

Another example is a student who eliminates distractions

like social media and video games during study time and avoids procrastination, will be able to study more effectively, and complete assignments and projects on time. This student would be more productive and would be more likely to achieve academic success. In summary, eliminating distractions and time-wasters can help individuals to stay focused and motivated, and increase their productivity and efficiency, which leads to better time management. It's important to keep in mind that it's not always possible to eliminate all distractions and time-wasters, but by identifying the most significant ones and taking steps to minimize them, you can make a big difference in your productivity.

4. *Managing Email and Communication Effectively*

Managing email and communication effectively can help in time management and productivity by reducing the time spent on non-essential tasks and allowing individuals to focus on important tasks. Effective email and communication management can include setting specific times for checking and responding to emails, organizing and prioritizing emails, and using tools to automate and streamline communication.

For example, a business owner who sets specific times during the day to check and respond to emails and uses tools to automate and streamline communication such as creating email templates and using a CRM will be able to focus on important tasks and complete them more efficiently than someone who is constantly checking and responding to email. This business owner would be more productive and would be able to achieve more in less time.

Another example, is a student who sets specific times during the day to check and respond to emails and uses tools to organize and prioritize emails such as using filters and labels, will be able to focus on studying and completing assignments more effectively than someone who is constantly checking and responding to emails. This student would be more productive and would be more likely to achieve academic success.

In summary, managing email and communication effectively can help individuals to stay organized, focused, and motivated, which leads to better time management and productivity. It's important to find the right balance between staying connected and being productive, it's also important to set boundaries and not let email and communication take over your time and attention.

5. *Using Technology to Automate Repetitive Tasks*

Using technology to automate repetitive tasks can help in time management and productivity by freeing up time and allowing individuals to focus on more important tasks. Automation can include using tools and software to automate repetitive tasks such as scheduling, data entry, and communication.

For example, a business owner who uses scheduling software to automate appointment scheduling and customer follow-up will be able to focus on more important tasks such as sales and marketing and complete them more efficiently than someone who is manually scheduling appointments and follow-up. This business owner would be more productive and would be able to achieve more in less time.

Another example, is a student who uses tools to automate repetitive tasks such as data entry and research, will be able to focus on studying and completing assignments more effectively than someone who is manually doing these tasks. This student would be more productive and would be more likely to achieve academic success.

In summary, using technology to automate repetitive tasks can help individuals to stay organized, focused, and motivated, which leads to better time management and productivity. It's important to find the right tools and software that fit your needs and automate the repetitive tasks that consume most of your time, so you can focus on more important tasks.

6. *Prioritizing Self-care and Rest*

Prioritizing self-care and rest can help in time management and productivity by improving physical and mental well-being, reducing stress, and increasing overall performance. Self-care can include activities such as exercise, meditation, and taking breaks.

For example, an entrepreneur who prioritizes self-care and rest by taking regular breaks throughout the day, incorporating physical activity and meditation into their routine, will be able to focus on their work more effectively, be more creative, and have a better decision-making ability than someone who does not prioritize self-care. This entrepreneur would be more productive and would be able to achieve more in less time. Another example is a student who prioritizes self-care and rest by taking regular breaks throughout the day, incorporating physical activity and meditation into their routine will be able to focus on their studies more effectively, retain information better, and have a better memory than someone who does not prioritize self-care. This student would be more productive and would be more likely to achieve academic success.

In summary, Prioritizing self-care and rest can help individuals to stay focused, motivated, and energized, which leads to better time management and productivity. It's important to find balance, and make time for self-care and rest, so you can perform better and achieve your goals.

7. *Learning to Say "no" to Non-essential Commitments*

Learning to say "no" to non-essential commitments can help in time management and productivity by allowing individuals to focus on important tasks and avoid wasting time on non-essential activities. Saying "no" to non-

The Triumphant Mind – Success Rituals

essential commitments can help individuals to prioritize their time and energy, and avoid over-committing and becoming overwhelmed. For example, a business owner who learns to say "no" to non-essential commitments such as attending non-essential meetings or taking on non-essential projects, will be able to focus on important tasks such as growing their business and increasing revenue. This business owner would be more productive and would be able to achieve more in less time.

Another example is a student who learns to say "no" to non-essential commitments such as attending non-essential social events or taking on non-essential extracurricular activities will be able to focus on important tasks such as studying and completing assignments. This student would be more productive and would be more likely to achieve academic success.

In summary, learning to say "no" to non-essential commitments can help individuals to stay focused, motivated, and prioritize their time and energy, which leads to better time management and productivity. It's important to find balance and not overcommit yourself, so you can focus on what is important and achieve your goals.

8. *Breaking up Large tasks into Smaller, Manageable Chunks*

Breaking up large tasks into smaller, manageable chunks can help in time management and productivity by making tasks more manageable, reducing procrastination, and increasing motivation. By breaking up large tasks into smaller, more manageable chunks, individuals can focus on one task at a time, set specific deadlines, and track progress. For example, a business owner who breaks up a large project into smaller, manageable chunks, such as researching, planning, and executing, will be able to focus on one task at a time, set specific deadlines and track progress. This business owner would be more productive and would be able to achieve more in less time.

Another example is a student who breaks up a large research paper into smaller, manageable chunks such as researching, outlining, writing, and editing and will be able to focus on one task at a time, set specific deadlines and track progress. This student would be more productive and would be more likely to achieve academic success.

In summary, breaking up large tasks into smaller, manageable chunks can help individuals to stay organized, focused, motivated, and track progress which leads to better time management and productivity. It's important to find the right balance between breaking a task into smaller chunks, and not breaking it down to the point where you end up spending too much time on planning instead of executing.

9. Using Techniques that can boost Focus and Concentration

Using techniques that can boost focus and concentration can help in time management and productivity by allowing individuals to work more efficiently and effectively on important tasks. Several techniques can boost focus and concentration such as meditation, mindfulness, taking breaks, and using the Pomodoro Technique.

For example, a business owner who uses mindfulness techniques such as taking regular breaks and practicing meditation will be able to focus on their work more effectively, be more creative, and have a better decision-making ability than someone who does not use these techniques. This business owner would be more productive and would be able to achieve more in less time. Another example is a student who uses the Pomodoro Technique to break up their study time into 25-minute intervals, with short breaks in between, will be able to focus on their studies more effectively, retain information better, and have a better memory than someone who does not use this technique. This student would be more productive and would be more likely to achieve academic success.

In summary, using techniques that can boost focus and concentration can help individuals to stay focused, and motivated and increase their productivity and efficiency, which leads to better time management. It's important to find the techniques that work best for you and adapt them to your lifestyle.

10. Constantly Reviewing and Adjusting your Time Management Strategies

Constantly reviewing and adjusting your time management strategies can help in time management and productivity by allowing individuals to identify what works and what doesn't, and make necessary adjustments to improve their performance. Reviewing and adjusting your strategies can help to ensure that you are using the most effective methods and tools, and making the most of your time.

For example, a business owner who regularly reviews their time management strategies and makes adjustments as needed, such as trying new tools and techniques, will be able to improve their performance and achieve their goals more efficiently than someone who does not review and adjust their strategies.

Another example is a student who regularly reviews their time management strategies, such as studying schedule and techniques, and adjusts as needed, will be able to improve their performance and achieve their academic goals more efficiently than someone who does not review and adjust their strategies.

In summary, constantly reviewing and adjusting your time management strategies can help individuals to stay organized, focused, motivated, and make the most of their time, which leads to better time management and productivity. It's important to regularly review your strategies, identify what works and what doesn't, and make necessary adjustments to improve your performance and achieve your goals.

11. Delegating Tasks to Others

Delegating tasks to others can help in time management and productivity by allowing individuals to focus on important tasks and avoid wasting time on non-essential activities. Delegating tasks can also help to increase the overall efficiency and effectiveness of a team or organization.

For example, a business owner who delegates tasks such as customer service, data entry, and bookkeeping to other team members, will be able to focus on important tasks such as sales and marketing and complete them more efficiently than someone who is trying to handle all the tasks by themselves. This business owner would be more productive and would be able to achieve more in less time.

Another example is a manager who delegates tasks to their team members, such as planning, research, and execution will be able to focus on important tasks such as decision-making and strategy and complete them more efficiently than someone who is trying to handle all the tasks by themselves. This manager would be more productive and would be able to achieve more in less time.

In summary, delegating tasks to others can help individuals to stay focused, motivated, and prioritize their time and energy, which leads to better time management and productivity. It's important to find the right balance between delegating tasks and keeping control over the important ones, also it's important to choose the right person for the task, and provide clear instructions and guidance.

12. Batching similar tasks Together

Batching similar tasks together can help in time management and productivity by allowing individuals to focus on one type of task at a time, reduce mental fatigue and increase efficiency. By grouping similar tasks, individuals can avoid the time and energy spent on switching between different types of tasks.

For example, a business owner who batches similar tasks such as responding to customer emails, returning phone calls, and following up on leads together, will be able to focus on one type of task at a time and complete them more efficiently than someone who is switching between different types of tasks. This business owner would be more productive and would be able to achieve more in less time.

Another example, is a student who batches similar tasks such as studying for different subjects, together in one study session, will be able to focus on one type of task at a time, and retain information better than someone who is switching between different types of tasks. This student would be more productive and would be more likely to achieve academic success.

In summary, batching similar tasks together can help individuals to stay focused, and motivated, and increase efficiency which leads to better time management and productivity. It's important to find the right balance between batching tasks and not overloading yourself with too much of the same type of task at once, also it's important to schedule breaks in between batches to avoid burnout and maintain a good work-life balance.

13. Using a Task manager or Planner

Using a task manager or planner can help in time management and productivity by allowing individuals to organize, prioritize, and track their tasks and goals. A task manager or planner can help individuals to stay on top of their to-do list, set deadlines, and track progress.

For example, a business owner who uses a task manager or planner to organize, prioritize, and track their tasks and goals, will be able to focus on important tasks, set deadlines, and track progress. This business owner would be more productive and would be able to achieve more in less time.

Another example is a student who uses a task manager or planner to organize, prioritize, and track their tasks and goals, such as assignments and exams, and will be able to focus on important tasks, set deadlines, and track progress. This student would be more productive and would be more likely to achieve academic success.

In summary, using a task manager or planner can help

individuals to stay organized, focused, and motivated and track progress, which leads to better time management and productivity. It's important to find the right tool or method that works best for you, whether it's a physical planner, a digital app, or a combination of both. There are many different options available, so you can choose the one that best suits your needs and preferences.

14. Using a Calendar

Using a calendar to schedule regular check-ins and reviews can help in time management and productivity by allowing individuals to track progress, identify areas for improvement, and make adjustments as needed. By scheduling regular check-ins and reviews, individuals can stay on top of their goals and tasks, and ensure that they are making the most of their time.

For example, a business owner who uses a calendar to schedule regular check-ins and reviews of their business plan, goals, and tasks, will be able to track progress, identify areas for improvement, and make adjustments as needed. This a business owner would be more productive and would be able to achieve more in less time.

Another example, is a student who uses a calendar to schedule regular check-ins and reviews of their academic goals and tasks, will be able to track progress, identify areas for improvement, and make adjustments as needed.

This student would be more productive and would be

more likely to achieve academic success.

In summary, using a calendar to schedule regular check-ins and reviews can help individuals to stay organized, focused, and motivated and track progress, which leads to better time management and productivity. It's important to schedule regular check-ins and reviews, whether it's daily, weekly, or monthly, to ensure that you are making the most of your time and achieving your goals.

15. Building good Habits and Routines

Building good habits and routines can help in time management and productivity by allowing individuals to establish a consistent schedule, reduce decision fatigue and increase efficiency. Habits and routines can help individuals to prioritize their time, focus on important tasks, and stay on track with their goals.

For example, a business owner who builds good habits and routines such as, starting the day with a set of prioritized tasks, and taking regular breaks, will be able to establish a consistent schedule, reduce decision fatigue and increase efficiency. This business owner would be more productive and would be able to achieve more in less time.

Another example is a student who builds good habits and routines such as, starting the day with a set of prioritized tasks, and studying at the same time every day, will be able to establish a consistent schedule, reduce decision fatigue and increase efficiency. This student would be more productive and would be more likely to achieve academic success.

In summary, Building good habits and routines can help individuals to stay organized, focused, motivated, and increase efficiency, which leads to better time management and productivity. It's important to find the right balance between consistency and flexibility, and build habits that align with your goals and lifestyle. Also, it's important to make them sustainable, by starting small, being consistent, and gradually increasing the complexity of the habits.

Networking and Building Relationships

Overview

- ❖ *Role of Networking and Building Relationships*
- ❖ *Effective Ways to Build Networks and Relationships*
    - ✓ *Building Authentic Connections*
    - ✓ *Active Listening and Showing Interest*
    - ✓ *Offering Help and Assistance*
    - ✓ *Following Up with Contacts*
    - ✓ *Expanding Network*
    - ✓ *Participating in Networking Events and Professional Organizations*
    - ✓ *Maintaining Regular Communication*
    - ✓ *Taking the Initiative to Connect*
    - ✓ *Being a Good Communicator*
    - ✓ *Showing Appreciation and Giving Back*

ROLE OF NETWORKING AND BUILDING RELATIONSHIPS

Networking and building relationships play a significant role in achieving success. Networking is the process of building and maintaining relationships with people who can help you achieve your goals. Building relationships with the right people can provide access to valuable resources, knowledge, and opportunities that can help you to achieve your goals.

Networking allows individuals to connect with potential mentors, collaborators, and partners who can provide guidance and support in different areas. For example, a business owner who builds relationships with other business owners can gain access to valuable insights, knowledge, and opportunities that can help them to grow their business and increase revenue.

Networking also allows individuals to expand their professional and personal networks, which can lead to new job opportunities, career advancement, and increased visibility in their industry. For example, a student who builds relationships with professionals in their field of interest can gain access to job opportunities and mentorship that can help them to achieve their career goals.

In summary, networking and building relationships are key factors in achieving success. Networking enables individuals to gain access to valuable resources, knowledge, and opportunities that can help them to achieve their goals and advance in their careers. It's important to actively seek out and nurture relationships with people who can help you achieve your goals and be open to opportunities and collaborations.

EFFECTIVE WAYS TO BUILD NETWORKS AND RELATIONSHIPS

Effective ways to build networks and strong relationships include:

1. Building Authentic Connections

Building authentic connections is an effective way to build a network and strong relationships because it allows for mutual trust and understanding to develop. When people feel that they can be themselves around each other and that their thoughts and feelings are valued, they are more likely to want to invest time and energy into the relationship.

For example, imagine a business professional who regularly attends networking events but only talks about their work and never asks others about their interests or hobbies. They may be able to make some connections, but they will likely be surface-level and not very meaningful. On the other hand, if that same person takes the time to get to know the people and they meet and shows genuine interest in their lives, they are much more likely to form strong, authentic connections that could lead to mutually beneficial business opportunities in the future.

2. *Active Listening and Showing Interest*

Active listening and showing interest are effective ways to build a network and strong relationships because they demonstrate that you value the other person and are invested in the conversation. When someone feels heard and understood, they are more likely to open up and share more about themselves, which can lead to a deeper connection.

For example, imagine two colleagues who work together in the same department. One of the colleagues is an active listener and regularly asks the other about their life, their interests, and goals, and genuinely shows interest in their responses. As a result, the other colleague feels valued and appreciated, and they become friends. They develop a close working relationship that leads to better collaboration, productivity, and job satisfaction. The colleague who actively listens and shows interest is more likely to be trusted, respected, and recommended by the other colleague, which can be beneficial to their career development.

3. *Offering Help and Assistance*

Offering help and assistance is an effective way to build a network and strong relationships because it demonstrates that you are willing to go above and beyond to support the other person. When someone feels that they can rely on you and that you have their best interests at heart, they are more likely to want to invest time and energy into the relationship. For example, imagine a young professional who has recently started a new job. They are struggling to understand a particular aspect of their role and feeling overwhelmed. A senior colleague who has experience in the same field takes notice and offers to help. They spend time explaining the concept, providing resources, and even spending time mentoring the new employee. As a result, the new employee feels supported and valued, and they begin to develop strong relationships with their colleague. They begin to see their colleague as a mentor and someone they can rely on for guidance in the future. This colleague is more likely to be trusted, respected, and recommended by the new employee, which can be beneficial to the mentor's career development.

4. *Following Up with Contacts*

Following up with contacts is an effective way to build a network and strong relationships because it demonstrates that you value the other person and are invested in maintaining the connection. When someone feels that you remember them and that you are willing to take the initiative to reach out, they are more likely to want to invest time and energy into the relationship.

For example, imagine you meet someone at a networking event whom you hit it off with and share a common interest. If you follow up with them after the event, maybe by sending them an email or connecting with them on LinkedIn, they will appreciate that you took the time to remember them. You can even mention something that you talked about during the event to remind them of the connection. By following up, you are showing that you are interested in building a relationship and that you want to keep in touch. It will increase the likelihood of them responding to your message and making a strong connection. It also allows you to get to know the person better, and you can explore possibilities of working together in the future.

5. *Expanding Your Network*

Expanding your network is an effective way to build a network and strong relationships because it allows you to connect with more people who may have different perspectives, skills, and resources that can be beneficial to you. The more people you know, the more opportunities you have to find the right people to help you achieve your goals.

For example, imagine a small business owner who wants to expand their customer base. If they only network within their immediate circle of friends and family, they may miss out on potential customers who could be interested in their products or services. However, if they actively expand their network by attending industry events, joining local business organizations, and connecting with people online, they increase their chances of meeting people who can help them grow their business. By expanding their network, the business owner gets to know a diverse group of people who can provide valuable insights, resources, and leads. This can help them to identify new business opportunities and potentially grow their customer base.

6. *Participating in Networking Events and Professional Organizations*

Participating in networking events and professional organizations is an effective way to build a network and strong relationships because it allows you to connect with other professionals in your field who may have similar interests and goals. These events and organizations provide opportunities to meet new people, exchange ideas, and learn about new developments in your industry. They also help you to establish yourself as a leader in your field and can enhance your professional reputation.

For example, imagine a software engineer who wants to advance their career and stay current with the latest technology. If they only network within their immediate workplace, they may miss out on potential job opportunities, or new technologies that are being used in the industry.

However, if they actively participate in networking events and professional organizations that cater to software engineers, they can increase their chances of meeting people who can help them achieve their career goals.

By attending conferences, joining a professional association, and participating in local meetups, the software engineer gets to know a diverse group of people who can provide valuable insights, resources, and leads. This can help them to identify new job opportunities, learn about new technologies, and stay current with industry trends.

7. *Maintaining Regular Communication*

Maintaining regular communication is an effective way to build a network and strong relationships because it helps to keep the connection alive and strengthen the bond between individuals. By staying in touch with people regularly, you can keep them updated on what's happening in your life and your business, and in return, they will do the same.

This regular communication will help to build trust and understanding, making it easier for you to ask for help and support when you need it.

For example, imagine a salesperson who wants to build strong relationships with their clients. If they only communicate with their clients when they need something or when they want to close a deal, their clients may feel used and not valued.

However, if they maintain regular communication with their clients by sending them updates, relevant articles, or even just sending a quick "hello" message, their clients will feel valued, and the salesperson will be able to build trust and a strong relationship with them.

This regular communication keeps the clients informed about the salesperson's business and the salesperson informed about the client's needs and preferences. This can help the salesperson to identify new sales opportunities and serve their clients better.

8. Taking the Initiative to Connect

Taking the initiative to connect is an effective way to build a network and strong relationships because it demonstrates that you are proactive, interested, and invested in building a connection. When you take the initiative to connect with someone, it can show that you value them and their time, and it can make it easier for the other person to reciprocate.

For example, imagine a recent college graduate who is looking for job opportunities in their field. If they wait for potential employers to reach out to them, they may miss out on valuable opportunities. However, if they take the initiative to connect with potential employers by reaching out to them via email or LinkedIn, they increase their chances of being noticed and getting hired. By taking the initiative to connect with potential employers, the recent graduate is showing that they are interested in the company and the role and that they are proactive in their job search. This also allows them to get to know the employer better, and they can tailor their application accordingly to increase their chances of getting hired.

This initiative can help recent graduates to stand out from the competition and increase their chances of getting a job.

9. Being a Good Communicator

Being a good communicator is an effective way to build a network and strong relationships because it allows you to effectively convey your thoughts, ideas, and intentions to others. Good communication skills can help you to build trust and understanding with others, as well as establish yourself as a credible and reliable source of information. For example, imagine a project manager who is leading a team of people from different backgrounds and cultures. If the project the manager is not a good communicator, which can lead to confusion, delays, and misunderstandings among the team members. However, if the project manager is a good communicator, they can effectively convey expectations, goals, and ideas to the team. They can also actively listen to the team members and address any concerns or questions that they might have. By being a good communicator, the project manager can build trust, understanding, and respect among the team, which can help to improve team dynamics, and productivity and ensure the success of the project.

Being a good communicator is a valuable skill that can help you to build and maintain strong relationships in any area of your life, whether it be in your personal or professional life. It allows you to effectively convey your thoughts, ideas, and intentions to others, and in turn, helps you to build trust and understanding with others.

10. Showing Appreciation and Giving Back

Showing appreciation and giving back is an effective way to build a network and strong relationships because it demonstrates that you value the other person and are willing to invest time and energy in the relationship. When you show appreciation and give back, it can make the other person feel valued and appreciated, which can lead to deeper and more meaningful connections.

For example, imagine a business owner who has a loyal customer base. If the business owner only focuses on making sales and never shows appreciation or gives back to their customers, the customers may feel taken for granted and be less likely to continue doing business with them.

However, if the business owner shows appreciation by offering discounts, sending thank you notes, or hosting events for their customers, they can demonstrate that they value their customers and are invested in building a relationship with them. By giving back to their customers, the business owner can establish a positive reputation and foster long-term customer loyalty.

Showing appreciation and giving back can be done in many ways and it can be tailored to the situation and the relationship. It can be a small gesture or a big one, but what matters is the intention behind it. It's a way of showing that you value the other person and that you are willing to invest in the relationship. It can be very effective in building and maintaining strong relationships.

Personal Development

Overview

- ❖ *Introduction*
- ❖ *Essential Skills for Personality Development*
  - ✓ *Self-awareness*
  - ✓ *Emotional Intelligence*
  - ✓ *Communication*
  - ✓ *Interpersonal Skills*
  - ✓ *Adaptability*
  - ✓ *Confidence*
  - ✓ *Resilience*
  - ✓ *Goal Setting*
- ❖ *Need for a Charismatic Personality*
  - ✓ *Building Strong Relationships*
  - ✓ *Improving Communication Skills*
  - ✓ *Gaining Trust and Respect*
  - ✓ *Influencing Others*
  - ✓ *Inspiring Confidence*
  - ✓ *Enhancing Leadership Potential*
  - ✓ *Achieving Success in Career and Business*
  - ✓ *Overcoming Shyness and Insecurity*
  - ✓ *Enhancing Social Skills*
  - ✓ *Building a Positive Reputation*

INTRODUCTION

Personal development is a continuous process of self-improvement that involves setting and achieving goals, working on personal challenges, and taking steps to improve oneself in various areas such as mental, physical, and emotional well-being, as well as personal skills and abilities. It can include activities such as self-reflection, learning new things, and taking care of one's physical and mental health.

Personal development can take many different forms and can be approached in various ways, depending on the individual's needs and goals. For example, some people may focus on developing a specific skill or talent, while others may focus on improving their overall well-being.

Examples of personal development activities include:

- Taking a course or attending workshops to learn a new skill or improve upon an existing one.
- Setting and working towards personal goals such as saving money, getting in shape, or learning a new language.
- Engaging in self-reflection and journaling to gain insight into one's thoughts, feelings, and behaviors.
- Practicing mindfulness or meditation to improve mental and emotional well-being.
- Reading books or listening to podcasts on personal development topics to learn new ideas and strategies for self-improvement.

Personal development is a lifelong journey, and the most important thing is to be open-minded, curious, willing to learn new things and to be patient with oneself. It's important to remember that personal development is not about perfection, it's about becoming the best version of oneself, and it's a process that can be enjoyed, rather than seen as a chore.

ESSENTIAL SKILLS FOR PERSONALITY DEVELOPMENT

It is difficult to provide an exact number as it depends on the perspective from which one is looking at it. However, some commonly considered essential skills for personal development include:

1. Self-awareness

Self-awareness is an essential skill for personal development because it allows individuals to understand their thoughts, feelings, and behaviors, and how they influence their actions and reactions. It is the foundation for personal development, as it allows people to identify areas of improvement and make conscious choices about how they want to change. For example, if an individual is self-aware, they may notice that they tend to procrastinate.

This realization can allow them to take steps to change this behavior, such as setting specific deadlines for tasks, breaking large projects into smaller tasks, and using a planner to manage their time.

Self-awareness also enables people to understand their strengths and weaknesses, which can help them to set realistic goals and to identify the areas in which they need to improve. It also helps individuals to identify their values, beliefs, and priorities, which can guide them in making important decisions.

Furthermore, self-awareness can also help people to understand and manage their own emotions, which can be beneficial for their mental and emotional well-being. Self-awareness can help individuals to identify patterns in their emotional reactions, which can allow them to take steps to manage their emotions more effectively, such as practicing mindfulness or seeking professional help if necessary.

In summary, self-awareness is an essential skill for personal development as it allows individuals to understand themselves better and to make conscious choices about how they want to change, which is the foundation of personal development, it guides individuals in setting goals and making important decisions.

2. *Emotional Intelligence*

Emotional intelligence (EI) is an essential skill for personal development because it involves the ability to understand and manage one's own emotions, as well as the emotions of others. Emotionally intelligent individuals can not only recognize, understand, and manage their own emotions healthily, but they can also understand and respond to the emotions of others, which can be beneficial in a wide range of social and professional settings.

For example, an individual with high emotional intelligence may be able to identify when they are feeling stressed and take steps to manage that stress in a healthy way, such as going for a walk or practicing mindfulness. They may also be able to recognize when a colleague is feeling stressed and offer support or help to manage that stress.

Emotional intelligence can also be beneficial in the workplace, as individuals with high EI are often able to build strong relationships with their colleagues and can be effective leaders and team members. They can understand and respond to the emotions of others, which can be beneficial for communication and collaboration. They also can be effective in resolving conflicts and building a positive work environment.

In summary, Emotional Intelligence is an essential skill for personal development because it enables individuals to understand and manage their own emotions and the emotions of others. This can be beneficial in personal and professional settings, helping people to build strong relationships, communicate effectively, and create a positive work environment.

3. Communication

Communication is an essential skill for personal development because it allows individuals to express themselves clearly and effectively, both verbally and in writing. Good communication skills can be beneficial in a wide range of personal and professional settings, as they enable people to share their ideas, thoughts, and feelings in a way that is understood by others.

For example, an individual with strong communication skills may be able to effectively negotiate a raise or a promotion at work. They would be able to express their qualifications, accomplishments, and reasons why they deserve the raise or promotion clearly and convincingly. They also would be able to listen to and understand the perspectives of their employer or manager, which can be beneficial for finding a mutually beneficial solution.

Communication skills can also be beneficial in building and maintaining relationships, both personal and professional. For example, an individual with strong communication skills would be able to express their needs and wants in a relationship, as well as listen to and understand the perspective of their partner.

In summary, Communication is an essential skill for personal development because it enables individuals to express themselves clearly and effectively, both verbally and in writing. It allows people to share their ideas, thoughts, and feelings in a way that is understood by others and this can be beneficial in a wide range of personal and professional settings. Strong communication skills can lead to effective negotiation, building and maintaining relationships, and successful teamwork.

4. Interpersonal Skills

Interpersonal skills are essential for personal development because they involve the ability to interact effectively with others. These skills are important for building and maintaining relationships, both personal and professional. They can be beneficial in a wide range of settings, from the workplace to personal relationships.

An example of how interpersonal skills can be beneficial in personal development is when an individual has strong conflict-resolution skills. They may be able to identify and resolve conflicts in a relationship, whether it's with a partner, family member, or friend, healthily and constructively. Instead of avoiding the conflict, they might be able to express their feelings and needs while also listening to and understanding the perspective of the other person. This can lead to a deeper understanding and improved relationship between the parties involved.

In summary, Interpersonal skills are essential for personal development because they involve the ability to interact effectively with others. These skills are important for building and maintaining relationships, both personal and professional. They can be beneficial in a wide range of settings, from the workplace to personal relationships.

Examples of interpersonal skills include active listening, empathy, conflict resolution, teamwork, and negotiation.

5. *Adaptability*

Adaptability is an essential skill for personal development because it involves the ability to adjust to changing circumstances and to be open to new ideas and perspectives. Being adaptable allows individuals to be flexible and resilient in the face of challenges and changes, and to be able to adapt to new situations as they arise.

For example, an adaptable individual may be able to switch between multiple tasks or projects at work with ease and make adjustments to their work schedule as needed. They may also be open to new ideas and perspectives and able to adjust their ideas accordingly. This can be beneficial in the workplace, as it allows them to be responsive to changes and to adapt to new situations as they arise.

Adaptability can also be beneficial in personal relationships as well. For example, an adaptable individual may be able to adjust to the changing needs of their partner or children and be open to new ways of thinking about things. They may also be able to adapt to changes in their own life, such as starting a new job or moving to a new city, with greater ease.

In summary, adaptability is an essential skill for personal development because it involves the ability to adjust to changing circumstances and to be open to new ideas and perspectives. Being adaptable allows individuals to be flexible and resilient in the face of challenges and changes and to be able to adapt to new situations as they arise. This can be beneficial in both personal and professional settings, allowing individuals to be responsive to changes and adjust to new circumstances.

6. Confidence

Confidence is an essential skill for personal development because it involves having a belief in one's abilities and being self-assured. Confidence can help individuals to set and achieve goals, to take risks, and persevere in the face of challenges.

For example, an individual who is confident in their abilities may be more likely to take on new responsibilities at work, such as leading a team or taking on a new project. They would be more likely to speak up and express their ideas, even if they were different from others. They would also be more likely to take risks and try new things, which can lead to personal and professional growth.

Confidence can also be beneficial in personal relationships, as it can help individuals to express their needs and wants, set boundaries, and assert themselves when necessary. Confidence can also help individuals to be more resilient in the face of rejection or failure, as they believe in their abilities and are not discouraged by setbacks. It's important to note that confidence is not the same as arrogance or overconfidence. Confidence is a healthy belief in one's abilities and the ability to acknowledge one's limitations, while overconfidence is an excessive belief in one's abilities, which can lead to poor decision-making. In summary, Confidence is an essential skill for personal development because it involves having a belief in one's abilities and being self-assured. It can help individuals to set and achieve goals, to take risks, and persevere in the face of challenges, which can lead to personal and professional growth. It can also be beneficial in personal relationships, as it can help individuals to express their needs and wants, set boundaries, and assert themselves when necessary.

7. Resilience

Resilience is an essential skill for personal development because it involves the ability to bounce back from setbacks, handle stress, and maintain a positive outlook in the face of adversity. Resilience is the ability to adapt well to stress and to be able to cope with difficult situations without becoming overwhelmed.

For example, a resilient individual may be able to handle a challenging work project without becoming stressed or burned out. They would be able to maintain a positive outlook and find ways to overcome obstacles. They would also be able to bounce back from rejection or failure and learn from their experiences.

Resilience can also be beneficial in personal relationships, as it allows individuals to handle conflicts and challenges healthily, without becoming overwhelmed or giving up. They can maintain a positive outlook and find ways to move forward. It's important to note that resilience is a skill that can be learned and developed over time. Some people are naturally resilient, while others may need to work on developing resilience by learning new coping strategies and building a support network.

In summary, Resilience is an essential skill for personal development because it involves the ability to bounce back from setbacks, handle stress, and maintain a positive outlook in the face of adversity. It is the ability to adapt well to stress and to be able to cope with difficult situations without becoming overwhelmed. This skill can be beneficial in either personal or professional settings, allowing individuals to handle conflicts and challenges healthily, without becoming overwhelmed or giving up. Resilience can be learned and developed over time by learning new coping strategies and building a support network.

8. *Goal Setting*

Goal setting is an essential skill for personal development because it involves the ability to set clear and achievable goals and to develop a plan to achieve them. Setting goals allows individuals to focus their efforts, measure their progress, and feel a sense of accomplishment when they achieve their goals.

For example, an individual who sets a goal to lose weight

may create a plan that includes regular exercise, healthy eating, and tracking their progress. They would be able to measure their progress by tracking their weight loss and monitoring their fitness level. When they reach their goal, they will feel a sense of accomplishment and will have developed a habit of regular exercise and healthy eating.

Goal setting can also be beneficial in a professional setting, for example, an individual who sets a goal to get a promotion at work may create a plan that includes taking on additional responsibilities, building a network of contacts, and continuing their education. They will be able to track their progress and measure their efforts and when they get the promotion, they will feel a sense of accomplishment and have developed skills and habits that will continue to serve them well in the future.

It's important to note that goal setting is a continuous process, after achieving a goal, individuals need to set new goals to continue to grow and improve.

In summary, Goal setting is an essential skill for personal development because it involves the ability to set clear and achievable goals and to develop a plan to achieve them. Setting goals allows individuals to focus their efforts, measure their progress, and feel a sense of accomplishment when they achieve their goals.

This skill can be beneficial in both personal and professional settings and it's a continuous process that allows individuals to continue growing and improving.

NEED FOR A CHARISMATIC PERSONALITY

A charismatic personality can be beneficial for success in a variety of settings, as it can help individuals connect with others and build strong relationships. Charismatic individuals are often seen as confident, enthusiastic, and persuasive, which can make them effective leaders and communicators.

They can inspire others to follow their lead and be effective in motivating and energizing a team or group.

Additionally, charismatic people can be persuasive, which can be useful in several different contexts, such as sales, negotiation, and public speaking. They may also be more likely to be able to persuade others to see things from their point of view, which can be beneficial in a wide range of situations.

However, it is important to note that having a charismatic personality alone is not enough for success, and it is not the only trait that will lead to success. Other important factors include having a good work ethic, being knowledgeable and skilled in one's field, being able to work well with others, and having a strong sense of integrity.

Additionally, charisma can be learned and developed over time. Some people are naturally charismatic, but others can become more charismatic by learning new communication and social skills, as well as by developing a positive attitude and strong sense of self-confidence.

1. Building Strong Relationships

Building strong relationships plays a crucial role in personality development because it allows individuals to connect with others and gain new perspectives and insights. Strong relationships can provide support, encouragement, and a sense of belonging, which can help individuals grow and develop as individuals. For example, an individual who has a strong relationship with a mentor can gain valuable guidance and advice in their personal or professional life. A mentor can provide support and encouragement, as well as offer new perspectives and insights that can help the individual grow and develop as a person.

Building strong relationships can also be beneficial in a professional setting. For example, an individual who has strong relationships with their colleagues may be able to collaborate more effectively and build a positive work environment. They may also be more likely to receive support and guidance when needed, which can help them to advance in their career.

Building strong relationships can also be beneficial in personal life, for example, having a strong relationship with a partner or friend can provide emotional support and a sense of belonging, which can be beneficial for one's mental and emotional well-being.

In summary, building strong relationships play a crucial role in personality development because it allows individuals to connect with others and gain new perspectives and insights.

The Triumphant Mind – Success Rituals

Strong relationships can provide support, encouragement, and a sense of belonging, which can help individuals to grow and develop as individuals. This skill can be beneficial in both personal and professional settings, it provides support, guidance, and a sense of belonging, which can be beneficial for one's mental and emotional well-being.

2. *Improving Communication Skills*

Improving communication skills plays a significant role in personality development because it allows individuals to express themselves clearly and effectively, both verbally and in writing. Good communication skills can help people to build and maintain relationships, both personal and professional and can be beneficial in a wide range of settings, from the workplace to personal relationships.

Effective communication skills involve being able to express oneself clearly and listen actively, which can help to build trust and understanding with others. It also involves being able to adapt one's communication style to different situations and different people. Improving communication skills can help people to negotiate, collaborate, and resolve conflicts more effectively. In the workplace, good communication skills can be beneficial for building effective relationships with colleagues, supervisors, and clients. It can also help in networking, public speaking, and presentations. Clear and effective communication can help individuals to express their ideas and to be heard, which can lead to better decision-making, teamwork, and productivity.

In personal relationships, improving communication skills can help express needs and wants, build trust, and resolve conflicts. Good communication skills are important for building healthy relationships and maintaining positive self-esteem. In summary, improving communication skills play a significant role in personality development because it allows individuals to express themselves clearly and effectively, both verbally and in writing. Good communication skills can help people to build and maintain relationships.

3. *Gaining Trust and Respect*

Gaining trust and respect plays a crucial role in personality development because it is necessary for building and maintaining positive relationships, both personal and professional.

Trust and respect are essential for effective communication, teamwork, and leadership. When people trust and respect each other, they are more likely to listen to and consider each other's opinions and to work together effectively.

For example, an individual who has gained the trust and respect of their colleagues is more likely to be seen as a leader and to be selected for important projects or promotions. They will be more likely to be respected and followed by their colleagues, which can lead to a more positive and productive work environment.

In personal relationships, gaining trust and respect is important for building and maintaining healthy relationships. When people trust and respect each other, they are more likely to feel secure and valued in the relationship, which can lead to a more positive and fulfilling relationship.

Gaining trust and respect requires being trustworthy and respectful towards others, being honest, reliable, and consistent in words and actions. Showing empathy, being open-minded, and actively listening is also important in gaining the trust and respect of others.

In summary, gaining trust and respect plays a crucial role in personality development because it is necessary for building and maintaining positive relationships, both personal and professional. Trust and respect are essential for effective communication, teamwork, and leadership.

Gaining trust and respect requires being trustworthy and respectful towards others, being honest, reliable, and consistent in words and actions. Showing empathy, being open-minded, and actively listening is also important in gaining trust and respect from others.

4. Influencing Others

The ability to influence others plays a crucial role in personality development because it allows individuals to effectively communicate their ideas and perspectives, and to persuade others to take action. The ability to influence others can be beneficial in a wide range of personal and professional settings, from the workplace to personal relationships.

For example, in the workplace, an individual who can influence others can be an effective leader, able to inspire and motivate their team. They can also be effective in persuasion and negotiation, which can be beneficial for closing deals or getting buy-in for new projects or ideas.

In personal relationships, an individual who can influence others can be more effective in building and maintaining healthy relationships. They can be more successful in resolving conflicts and achieving their goals. They can also be more effective in mentoring and guiding others.

Influencing others requires good communication skills, the ability to build and maintain relationships, and the ability to understand and respond to the perspectives and motivations of others. It also requires being able to adapt one's communication style to different situations and different people, and being able to present ideas and perspectives compellingly and persuasively.

In summary, the ability to influence others plays a crucial role in personality development because it allows individuals to effectively communicate their ideas and perspectives, and to persuade others to take action. This skill can be beneficial in a wide range of personal and professional settings, and it requires good communication skills, the ability to build and maintain relationships, and the ability to understand and respond to the perspectives and motivations of others. It also requires being able to adapt one's communication style and being able to present ideas compellingly and persuasively.

5. *Inspiring Confidence*

The ability to inspire confidence plays a crucial role in personality development because it allows individuals to build trust and respect with others, and to lead by example. When people have confidence in an individual, they are more likely to follow their lead and support their ideas and decisions.

For example, in a professional setting, an individual who inspires confidence in their colleagues and supervisors is more likely to be seen as a leader and to be selected for important projects or promotions. They will be more likely to be respected and followed by their colleagues, which can lead to a more positive and productive work environment.

In personal relationships, inspiring confidence is important for building and maintaining healthy relationships. When people have confidence in an individual, they are more likely to feel secure and valued in the relationship, which can lead to a more positive and fulfilling relationship.

Inspiring confidence requires being trustworthy and respectful towards others, being honest, reliable, and consistent in words and actions. Showing empathy, being open-minded, and actively listening is also important in inspiring confidence from others.

In summary, the ability to inspire confidence plays a crucial role in personality development because it allows individuals to build trust and respect with others, and to lead by example. When people have confidence in an individual, they are more likely to follow their lead and support their ideas and decisions. Inspiring confidence requires being trustworthy and respectful towards others, being honest, reliable, and consistent in words and actions. Showing empathy, being open-minded, and actively listening is also important in inspiring confidence from others.

6. *Enhancing Leadership Potential*

Enhancing leadership potential plays a crucial role in personality development because it allows individuals to effectively guide, motivate, and inspire others toward a common goal. Leadership skills can be beneficial in a wide range of personal and professional settings, from the workplace to community organizations, and can help individuals to make a positive impact in their communities and organizations.

Leadership potential can be enhanced by developing a range of skills including communication, problem-solving, decision-making, emotional intelligence, and goal-setting. A strong leader should be able to communicate effectively and inspire trust, be able to make difficult decisions and solve problems, be able to understand and manage their own emotions and those of others, and be able to set and achieve goals. For example, in a professional setting, an individual with strong leadership potential can be an effective leader, able to inspire and motivate their team, and guide them towards achieving their goals. This can lead to a more positive and productive work environment and can help the leader and the team to achieve their objectives.

In personal relationships, enhancing leadership potential can be beneficial in building and maintaining healthy relationships and achieving goals. A leader in their personal life can guide and motivate others, resolve conflicts, and make important decisions.

In summary, Enhancing leadership potential plays a crucial role in personality development because it allows individuals to effectively guide, motivate, and inspire others toward a common goal. Leadership skills can be beneficial in a wide range of personal and professional settings and can help individuals to make a positive impact in their communities and organizations.

7. *Achieving Success in Career and Business*

Achieving success in career and business plays a crucial role in personality development because it allows individuals to reach their full potential in terms of their professional goals and aspirations. Achieving success in a career or business can provide a sense of accomplishment, and financial stability and it can also open up new opportunities for personal and professional growth. To achieve success in a career and business, individuals need to develop a range of skills such as good communication, problem-solving, adaptability, goal setting, and effective time management. They should also be able to build and maintain professional relationships, be able to lead and manage others, and have the ability to think strategically, and make informed decisions.

For example, an individual who has achieved success in their career or business may have reached a high level in their profession, such as a senior executive or a business owner. They have built a reputation for excellence and have a strong network of professional contacts. They have also gained the skills and experience necessary to continue to grow and evolve in their field.

Achieving success in career and business can also have a positive impact on personal life, as it can provide financial stability, a sense of purpose, and a sense of accomplishment.

In summary, Achieving success in career and business plays a crucial role in personality development because it allows individuals to reach their full potential in terms of their professional goals and aspirations. Achieving success in a career or business can provide a sense of accomplishment, and financial stability and it can also open up new opportunities for personal and professional growth. To achieve success in career and business, individuals need to develop a range of skills such as good communication, problem-solving, adaptability, goal setting, and effective time management, and also have to be able to build and maintain professional relationships, lead and manage others, think strategically and make informed decisions.

8. Overcoming Shyness and Insecurity

Overcoming shyness and insecurity plays a crucial role in personality development because it allows individuals to build self-confidence, interact more effectively with others, and reach their full potential in personal and professional settings. Shyness and insecurity can hold people back from achieving their goals and from building positive relationships with others.

For example, an individual who is shy or insecure may have difficulty communicating with others or may avoid social situations altogether. This can make it difficult for them to build and maintain relationships, achieve their goals, and succeed in their personal and professional lives.

Overcoming shyness and insecurity requires developing self-confidence, learning effective communication skills, and building a positive self-image. This can be achieved through the therapy, self-help techniques, and support groups. It can also be achieved by setting small goals, gradually facing and overcoming fears, and practicing assertiveness and positive self-talk.

In summary, Overcoming shyness and insecurity plays a crucial role in personality development because it allows individuals to build self-confidence, interact more effectively with others, and reach their full potential in personal and professional settings. Shyness and insecurity can hold people back from achieving their goals and from building positive relationships with others. Overcoming shyness and insecurity requires developing self-confidence, learning effective communication skills, and building a positive self-image. This can be achieved through the therapy, self-help techniques, and support groups, by setting small goals and gradually facing and overcoming fears, and by practicing assertiveness and positive self-talk.

9. *Enhancing Social Skills*

Enhancing social skills plays a crucial role in personality development because it allows individuals to interact effectively with others, build and maintain positive relationships, and navigate social situations with ease. Good social skills can be beneficial in a wide range of personal and professional settings, from the workplace to personal relationships.

For example, in a professional setting, an individual with strong social skills can be effective in building and maintaining professional relationships, which can be beneficial for networking and building a positive work environment. They can also be more effective in teamwork, negotiation, and resolving conflicts.

In personal relationships, enhancing social skills can be beneficial in building and maintaining healthy relationships. Good social skills can help individuals to effectively communicate their needs and wants, to build trust, and to resolve conflicts.

Enhancing social skills involves being able to effectively communicate with others, being able to understand and respond to the perspectives and emotions of others, and being able to navigate social situations with ease. It also involves being able to adapt one's communication style to different situations and different people.

In summary, enhancing social skills plays a crucial role in personality development because it allows individuals to interact effectively with others, build and maintain positive relationships, and navigate social situations with ease. Good social skills can be beneficial in a wide range of personal and professional settings, from the workplace to personal relationships. Enhancing social skills involves being able to effectively communicate with others, and being able to understand and respond to the perspectives and emotions of others, and being able to navigate social situations with ease. It also involves being able to adapt one's communication style to different situations and different people.

10. Building a Positive Reputation

Building a positive reputation plays a crucial role in personality development because it allows individuals to establish trust and credibility with others, and to be viewed as a reliable and respected members of their community or organization. A positive reputation can open up opportunities for personal and professional growth and can make it easier to achieve one's goals.

For example, in a professional setting, an individual with a positive reputation is more likely to be viewed as a leader and to be selected for important projects or promotions. They will be more likely to be respected and followed by their colleagues, which can lead to a more positive and productive work environment.

In personal relationships, building a positive reputation can be beneficial in building and maintaining healthy relationships. When people have a positive perception of an individual, they are more likely to feel secure and valued in the relationship, which can lead to a more positive and fulfilling relationship.

Building a positive reputation requires being trustworthy and respectful towards others, honest, reliable, and consistent in words and actions. Showing empathy, being open-minded, and actively listening is also important in building a positive reputation.

In summary, Building a positive reputation plays a crucial role in personality development because it allows individuals to establish trust and credibility with others, and to be viewed as a reliable and respected members of their community or organization. A positive reputation can open up opportunities for personal and professional growth and make it easier to achieve one's goals. Building a positive reputation requires being trustworthy and respectful towards others, being honest, reliable, and consistent in words and actions, showing empathy, being open-minded, and actively listening.

Leadership and Communication

Overview

- ❖ *Significance of Leadership and Communication*
- ❖ *Improving Leadership Qualities*
    - ✓ *Self-reflection*
    - ✓ *Communication*
    - ✓ *Emotional Intelligence*
    - ✓ *Continuous Learning*
    - ✓ *Lead by Example*
- ❖ *Broadening Communication Skills*
    - ✓ *Listen Actively*
    - ✓ *Speak Clearly and Confidently*
    - ✓ *Use Nonverbal Communication*
    - ✓ *Be Aware of the Audience*
    - ✓ *Practice*

SIGNIFICANCE OF LEADERSHIP AND COMMUNICATION

Leadership and communication are both important for the success of any organization and group.

Leadership sets the direction and vision for the group and communicates it effectively to the members. A leader who can clearly articulate a vision and inspire others to work towards it can help to focus the efforts of the group and achieve greater results.

For example, Steve Jobs was a charismatic leader who was able to communicate his vision for Apple and inspire his employees to innovate and create revolutionary products.

Effective communication is also critical for maintaining cohesion and cooperation within a group. A leader who can effectively listen to and address the concerns and ideas of team members can help to build trust and foster a positive work environment.

For example, the ex-CEO of Patagonia, Rose Marcario, is known for her open-door policy and encourages employees to share their ideas and concerns to help make the company more sustainable and socially responsible.

IMPROVING LEADERSHIP QUALITIES

There are several ways to improve leadership qualities, including:

1. Self-reflection

Self-reflection is an important tool for improving leadership qualities as it allows individuals to step back and evaluate their actions and behaviors. Through self-reflection, leaders can gain a deeper understanding of their strengths and weaknesses and identify areas for improvement. This can lead to more effective decision-making, better communication, and improved relationships with team members.

An example of how self-reflection can improve leadership qualities is when a manager takes the time to reflect on their communication style with their team. Through self-reflection, the manager may realize that they tend to be too directive and do not give their team enough autonomy. By recognizing this and making a conscious effort to give their team more independence, the manager can build trust and improve their team's engagement, which can lead to better performance and productivity.

Additionally, self-reflection can improve emotional intelligence and empathy, which are crucial traits for successful leaders. Self-reflection can also help leaders to acknowledge their own biases, and prejudices and how they affect their leadership style and relationships. This awareness can help them to be more inclusive, diverse, and equitable.

Overall, self-reflection can be an effective tool for leaders to continuously improve themselves and their leadership style, which in turn can lead to better performance and effectiveness in their role.

2. *Communication*

Effective communication is a key component of strong leadership, as it helps leaders to convey their vision and goals, build trust, and motivate their team. Good communication skills are essential for leaders to build and maintain relationships, resolve conflicts, and make informed decisions.

An example of how communication improves leadership qualities is a leader who consistently holds team meetings to keep team members informed about company developments, new policies, and upcoming projects. By regularly communicating with the team, the leader can build trust and keep the team informed, which can lead to better performance and higher job satisfaction.

Effective communication also includes active listening, being able to understand and interpret others' perspectives, and constructively giving feedback. A leader who is an effective communicator can create a positive work environment and foster collaboration among team members.

Additionally, a leader who can communicate clearly, concisely, and persuasively can convey their vision and goals effectively and gain buy-in from their team, stakeholders, and the organization. They can also communicate the progress and results to the team and other stakeholders, which can help build trust and credibility. Overall, effective communication is an essential quality of a good leader, as it helps to build trust, motivate team members and create a positive work environment.

3. *Emotional Intelligence*

Emotional intelligence (EI) refers to the ability to recognize, understand, and manage one's own emotions and those of others. EI is an important leadership quality as it helps leaders to effectively communicate, make decisions, and build relationships.

An example of how emotional intelligence improves leadership qualities is a leader who can manage their own emotions in a difficult situation. For example, a leader who can remain calm and composed during a crisis can help to keep the team focused and prevent them from becoming overwhelmed. This can help to maintain productivity and make better decisions.

Emotional intelligence also includes the ability to empathize with others, which is crucial for building strong relationships with team members. A leader who can understand and respond to the emotions of their team members can create a positive work environment, foster collaboration, and build trust.

Additionally, emotionally intelligent leaders can recognize and manage emotions in others, which can help them to resolve conflicts, give feedback, and build a more inclusive and diverse work environment. They can also create a culture of psychological safety, where team members feel comfortable expressing their ideas and opinions. Overall, emotional intelligence is an essential quality of a good leader, as it helps to build strong relationships, make better decisions, and create a positive and inclusive work environment.

4. *Continuous Learning*

Continuous learning is an important quality of a good leader, as it helps them to stay current with the latest trends, technologies, and best practices in their field, as well as to develop new skills and capabilities. This helps leaders to better understand the needs and challenges of their team and organization and to make more informed decisions.

An example of how continuous learning improves leadership qualities is a leader who takes the time to regularly attend industry conferences and networking events, read relevant books and articles and take online courses or professional development programs. By staying current with the latest trends and best practices, this leader can identify new opportunities for their organization and make better decisions. Continuous learning also includes seeking feedback, taking accountability for mistakes, and reflecting on one's leadership style. A leader who is willing to reflect on their performance and seek feedback can identify areas for improvement and continuously develop their leadership skills.

Additionally, continuous learning helps leaders to stay

adaptable to changes and to be open to new ideas, perspectives, and ways of working. This helps to foster innovation and creativity within the team and the organization.

Overall, continuous learning is an essential quality of a good leader, as it helps to stay current with the latest trends and best practices, continuously develop leadership skills, and foster innovation and adaptability.

5. Lead by Example

Leading by example is a key leadership quality that helps leaders to gain the trust and respect of their team members. By setting a positive example through their actions and behaviors, leaders can inspire their teams to strive for excellence and to adhere to the same standards of excellence.

An example of how leading by example improves leadership qualities is a leader who consistently arrives to work on time, meets deadlines, and maintains a positive attitude. By doing so, this leader sets a standard of punctuality and reliability for the team to follow, and this can help to increase productivity and job satisfaction.

Leading by example also includes being transparent, honest, and accountable. A leader who is willing to admit their mistakes and take responsibility for their actions can build trust and credibility with their team. Additionally, a leader who is transparent and open with communication can create a culture of trust and accountability within the team.

Additionally, leading by example means, walking the talk, being consistent, and practicing what is being preached. This can help to create a culture of integrity, commitment, and motivation within the team.

Overall, leading by example is an essential quality of a good leader, as it helps to gain the trust and respect of team members, set a positive example, and create a culture of excellence and accountability.

BROADENING COMMUNICATION SKILLS

There are many ways to boost your communication skills, including:

1. Listen Actively

Active listening is an important skill that can enhance communication by allowing individuals to fully understand and engage with what is being said. It involves paying attention to the speaker, understanding their message, and responding in an appropriate and meaningful way. An example of how active listening can enhance communication skills is a manager who takes the time to listen to the concerns and ideas of their team members during a meeting. By actively listening, the manager can fully understand the perspectives of their team members, which can lead to better decision-making and problem-solving. Additionally, by actively listening, the manager can also provide feedback and support, which can help to build trust and improve employee engagement.

Active listening also includes being non-judgmental, being attentive to verbal and non-verbal cues, and clarifying any confusion or misunderstandings. This can help to avoid any miscommunication and build more effective and efficient communication.

Additionally, active listening can help to build a more inclusive and diverse work environment. By actively listening to different perspectives, a leader can gain new insights and understanding, and make better decisions that are inclusive and equitable.

Overall, active listening is an essential skill that can enhance communication by allowing individuals to fully understand and engage with what is being said, build trust, improve decision-making and foster a more inclusive and diverse work environment.

2. *Speak Clearly and Confidently*

Speaking clearly and confidently is an important aspect of effective communication, as it helps to convey a message effectively and persuasively. When speaking clearly and confidently, individuals can articulate their thoughts and ideas in a way that is easy to understand, and they project a sense of authority and credibility.

An example of how speaking clearly and confidently can enhance communication skills is a salesperson who presents a product to a potential client. By speaking clearly and confidently, the salesperson can effectively convey the benefits of the product and build trust with the client, which can lead to a successful sale.

Speaking clearly and confidently also includes being aware of the audience, adjusting the language and tone accordingly, and being mindful of body language and non-verbal cues. This can help to build a connection and credibility with the audience and make communication more effective.

Additionally, speaking clearly and confidently can help to overcome stage fright and build self-confidence. By speaking clearly and confidently, an individual can express themselves in a more effective way, which can help to build a more positive self-image and overcome communication anxiety.

Overall, speaking clearly and confidently is an important aspect of effective communication that can help to convey a message effectively, and build trust, credibility, and self-confidence.

3. Use Nonverbal Communication

Nonverbal communication is a powerful tool that can enhance verbal communication by providing additional context and meaning. Nonverbal communication includes facial expressions, body language, and tone of voice, and it can convey emotions, attitudes, and intentions that may not be explicitly stated.

An example of how using nonverbal communication can enhance communication skills is a manager who gives a presentation to their team. By using confident body language, such as maintaining eye contact and speaking with a strong, steady voice, the manager can project a sense of authority and credibility, which can help to engage the team and make the presentation more effective. Using nonverbal communication also includes being aware of the audience, adjusting the language and tone accordingly, and being mindful of body language and non-verbal cues. This can help to build a connection and credibility with the audience and make communication more effective.

Additionally, using nonverbal communication can help to build trust and credibility. For example, maintaining eye contact, nodding, and smiling can help to show engagement and attentiveness in a conversation and make the other person feel heard and valued.

Overall, using nonverbal communication is an important aspect of effective communication that can help to convey additional context and meaning, and build trust, credibility, and engagement.

4. Be Aware of the Audience

Being aware of the audience is an essential aspect of effective communication, as it helps to tailor the message and delivery to the needs and preferences of the listeners.

This can help to build a connection and credibility with the audience and make communication more effective.

An example of how being aware of the audience can enhance communication skills is a manager who gives a presentation to a team of engineers.

By being aware of the audience, the manager can use technical language and provide detailed explanations that would be relevant and understandable for the engineers, which can help to engage them and make the presentation more effective.

Being aware of the audience also includes understanding the audience's perspective, expectations, and goals. This can help to adjust the message and delivery accordingly and make the communication more effective.

Additionally, being aware of the audience can help to create a more inclusive and diverse work environment, by understanding and addressing the needs and concerns of different groups within the audience.

Additionally, being aware of the audience can help to build trust and credibility. For example, addressing the audience by their name, showing understanding of their concerns, and tailoring the message to their needs can help to build a connection and trust with the audience.

Overall, being aware of the audience is an essential aspect of effective communication that can help to tailor the message and delivery, build trust and credibility, and create a more inclusive and diverse work environment.

5. *Practice*

Practice is an essential aspect of enhancing communication skills. Through practice, individuals can improve their ability to convey their message effectively and persuasively, build self-confidence, and become more comfortable in different communication situations.

An example of how practice can enhance communication skills is a manager who wants to improve their public speaking skills. By practicing delivering presentations in front of a mirror, or to a small group of colleagues, the manager can improve their delivery, gain feedback and become more comfortable and confident when speaking in front of a larger audience.

Practice also includes seeking feedback, and reflecting on one's performance. This can help to identify areas for improvement and continuously develop communication skills. Additionally, practicing different communication scenarios, such as giving feedback, presenting, or negotiating, can help to become more adaptable and effective in different situations.

Additionally, practice can help to overcome communication anxiety and build self-confidence. By practicing different communication scenarios, an individual can become more comfortable and confident in expressing themselves and overcome communication anxiety.

Overall, practice is an essential aspect of enhancing communication skills, it can help to improve delivery, gain feedback, become more adaptable and effective in different situations, overcome communication anxiety and build self-confidence.

Decision-making and Problem-Solving

Overview

- ❖ *The Importance of Decision-making and Problem-Solving Skills*
- ❖ *Strengthening Decision-making and Problem-solving Skills*
    - ✓ *Understanding the Decision-making Process*
    - ✓ *Identifying and Defining the Problem*
    - ✓ *Gathering and Analyzing Information*
    - ✓ *Identifying and Evaluating Alternatives*
    - ✓ *Considering the Consequences of Different Choices*
    - ✓ *Communicating and Collaborating with Others*
    - ✓ *Considering Ethical Implications*
    - ✓ *Managing Uncertainty and Risk*
    - ✓ *Developing a Plan of Action*
    - ✓ *Continuously Reflecting and Improving*

THE IMPORTANCE OF DECISION-MAKING AND PROBLEM-SOLVING SKILLS

Decision-making and problem-solving skills are important for leaders because they allow them to make effective decisions and find solutions to challenges that arise.

- *Decision-making*

Decision-making is the process of identifying and choosing alternatives based on the values and preferences of the decision-maker. Leaders need to make well-informed decisions that align with the goals of the organization and that consider the potential consequences. For example, a CEO might decide to invest in a new product line to increase revenue for the company.

- *Problem-solving*

Problem-solving is the process of identifying, analyzing, and solving problems. Effective problem-solving is an important skill for leaders because it allows them to identify and address challenges that arise within the organization. For example, a team leader might need to solve a problem of low morale among team members by identifying the root cause and implementing solutions such as team-building activities or improved communication.

Some more examples are:

- A manager at a manufacturing company uses problem-solving skills to identify the root cause of production delays and implement a solution to improve efficiency and meet deadlines.
- A leader in a non-profit organization uses decision-making skills to evaluate potential programs and chooses the one that aligns best with the organization's mission and has the potential to have the greatest impact.

STRENGTHENING DECISION-MAKING AND PROBLEM-SOLVING SKILLS

There are several ways to strengthen decision-making and problem-solving skills, including:

1. Understanding the Decision-making Process

Understanding the decision-making process can help individuals to make better decisions and solve problems more effectively. It involves identifying the problem, gathering and analyzing information, considering alternatives, making a decision, and evaluating the outcome.

An example of how understanding the decision-making process can strengthen decision-making and problem-solving skills is a manager who is facing a problem with high employee turnover. By identifying the problem, gathering information about the reasons for the turnover, considering alternatives such as offering better benefits or improving the work environment, making a decision to implement a new training program for managers, and then evaluating the outcome by monitoring the employee retention rate.

Additionally, understanding the decision-making process can help to include different perspectives, be more inclusive and diverse, and consider the long-term and short-term consequences of the decision. This can lead to more effective and equitable decision-making.

Furthermore, it can also help to be more mindful of biases, emotions, and assumptions that can impact the decision-making process, and make more deliberate and rational decisions.

Overall, understanding the decision-making process can help to make better decisions and solve problems more effectively, by identifying the problem, gathering and analyzing information, considering alternatives, making a decision, and evaluating the outcome in a more inclusive, diverse, and rational way.

2. *Identifying and Defining the Problem*

Properly identifying and defining a problem can strengthen decision-making and problem-solving skills by providing a clear understanding of the situation, what needs to be accomplished, and what resources are available. It can also help to identify potential obstacles and pitfalls.

For example, if a company is experiencing a decline in sales, it may initially believe that the problem is a lack of marketing. However, upon further investigation, they may find that the problem is a lack of product innovation and development. By properly identifying and defining the problem, the company can then focus on developing new products rather than just increasing its marketing efforts, which would have been an ineffective solution.

3. *Gathering and Analyzing Information*

Gathering and analyzing information can strengthen decision-making and problem-solving skills by providing a thorough understanding of the situation and all relevant factors. It allows for the identification of patterns, trends, and connections that can inform decisions and solutions.

For example, if a manager wants to increase efficiency in the manufacturing process, they would gather and analyze data on production output, machine downtime, labor hours, and inventory levels. By analyzing this information, they may discover that the majority of downtime is caused by a specific machine that needs maintenance. By identifying this pattern, the manager can decide to schedule regular maintenance on the machine and improve efficiency in the manufacturing process. Additionally, gathering and analyzing information allows one to weigh options and make an informed decision, which can help to avoid potential mistakes and negative consequences.

4. *Identifying and Evaluating Alternatives*

Identifying and evaluating alternatives can strengthen decision-making and problem-solving skills by providing a range of options to choose from, and by encouraging critical thinking and creativity. It allows one to consider the pros and cons of different options and select the one that best aligns with the goals and objectives.

For example, a school principal may be facing a problem of overcrowding in the school. Identifying and evaluating alternatives, the principal may consider options such as building a new school, renting additional classroom space, or implementing a schedule change. After evaluating each option, the principal may decide that the best solution is to rent additional classroom space, as it is the most cost-effective and quickest solution.

Additionally, identifying and evaluating alternatives helps one to be prepared for potential problems and to have backup plans in place. Also, it can help one to anticipate potential obstacles and challenges, and it allows one to make decisions that are more likely to be successful and produce positive outcomes.

5. *Considering the Consequences of Different Choices*

Considering the consequences of different choices can strengthen decision-making and problem-solving skills by helping to anticipate the potential short-term and long-term outcomes of different options. It allows one to weigh the costs and benefits of different choices and make an informed decision. For example, a small business owner is considering expanding the business by taking out a loan. They must consider the consequences of different choices: if they take out a loan, they will have more money to invest in the business, but they will also be taking on debt. However, if they don't take out a loan, they may miss out on an opportunity to grow the business. By considering the consequences, the owner can decide whether or not to take out a loan and how much debt they are willing to take on.

Additionally, considering the consequences of different choices allows one to plan for potential issues and to make decisions that are more likely to produce positive outcomes. It also allows one to take a more strategic and long-term approach to problem-solving and decision-making, which can lead to more effective solutions.

6. *Communicating and Collaborating with Others*

Communicating and collaborating with others can strengthen decision-making and problem-solving skills by providing different perspectives and ideas, and by increasing the amount of information and resources available. It allows one to gather input from a diverse group of people and to build support for a chosen solution.

For example, a city council is trying to solve the problem

of traffic congestion. By communicating and collaborating with others, they can gather input from city planners, transportation engineers, and community members. They can learn about different perspectives on the problem and gather ideas for possible solutions. Through collaboration, they may develop a comprehensive plan that addresses the problem from multiple angles, such as expanding public transportation, creating bike lanes, and encouraging carpooling.

Additionally, communicating and collaborating with others allows one to build a team, which can help to divide the workload and to achieve a common goal. It also allows one to foster a sense of shared ownership and accountability, which can lead to better decision-making and problem-solving.

7. Considering Ethical Implications

Considering ethical implications can strengthen decision-making and problem-solving skills by ensuring that the chosen course of action aligns with moral and ethical principles, and by anticipating potential negative consequences. It allows one to take a responsible and fair approach to problem-solving and decision-making.

For example, a company is considering outsourcing production to a foreign country where labor laws are less strict than in their home country. By considering the ethical implications, they would consider the potential negative effects on the workers such as low wages, poor working conditions, and a lack of job security. The company may then decide to invest in a more expensive, but the more ethical alternative, such as investing in automation to produce products in-house. Additionally, considering ethical implications can help to maintain the integrity and reputation of the organization, and it can help to ensure that the solution is sustainable in the long term. It also allows one to anticipate and mitigate any negative consequences that may arise from the decision, which can lead to more effective solutions.

8. Managing Uncertainty and Risk

Managing uncertainty and risk can strengthen decision-making and problem-solving skills by helping one to anticipate and prepare for potential challenges, and by allowing one to make decisions based on the best available information. It allows one to identify and mitigate potential risks and to plan for contingencies.

For example, a company is considering a new product launch. By managing uncertainty and risk, the company would conduct market research, assess the competition, and evaluate the product's profitability. They would also put in place a plan for handling potential issues such as low sales, supply chain disruptions, or product recalls.

By identifying and mitigating potential risks, the company can make a more informed decision about whether or not to launch the product and can plan for contingencies if things don't go as expected.

Additionally, managing uncertainty and risk allows one

to make decisions that are more likely to produce positive outcomes, and it helps to ensure that the solution is sustainable in the long term. It also allows one to anticipate and mitigate negative consequences that may arise from the decision, which can lead to more effective solutions.

9. Developing a Plan of Action

Developing a plan of action can strengthen decision-making and problem-solving skills by providing a clear and structured approach to implementing a solution. It allows one to break down a problem or a goal into smaller, manageable steps and assign specific tasks with deadlines.

For example, a team is tasked with reducing waste in a manufacturing facility. By developing a plan of action, they can first identify the sources of waste, prioritize areas that need improvement, and then develop specific strategies and action steps to address those areas. They could also assign specific tasks, set deadlines, and establish a system for monitoring progress and making adjustments as needed. By following the plan of action, the team can make steady progress toward their goal and can measure the effectiveness of their solution. Additionally, developing a plan of action allows one to stay focused and organized, and it helps to ensure that the solution is implemented efficiently and effectively. It also allows one to anticipate and mitigate any negative consequences that may arise from the decision, which can lead to more effective solutions.

10. Continuously Reflecting and Improving

Continuously reflecting and improving can strengthen decision-making and problem-solving skills by allowing one to evaluate the effectiveness of a solution and make adjustments as needed. It allows one to learn from past experiences and make better decisions in the future.

For example, a manager who had to deal with a customer complaint can reflect on how the situation was handled and identify areas for improvement. They may realize that they could have been more empathetic or could have provided a better solution to the customer's problem. By reflecting on the experience and identifying areas for improvement, the manager can take steps to prevent similar situations from occurring in the future and can improve their customer service skills.

Additionally, continuously reflecting and improving allows one to stay adaptable and responsive to change, and it helps to ensure that the solution is sustainable in the long term. It also allows one to learn from past experiences, which can lead to more effective solutions in the future.

The Triumphant Mind – Success Rituals

Creativity and Innovation

Overview

- ❖ *The Power of Creativity and Innovation*
- ❖ *Improving Creative Skills*
    - ✓ *Dedicating Time for Creativity*
    - ✓ *Keeping an Idea Journal*
    - ✓ *Broadening your Perspective*
    - ✓ *Taking Inspiration from Diverse Sources*
    - ✓ *Practicing Brainstorming Techniques*
    - ✓ *Playing with different Mediums and Techniques*
    - ✓ *Collaborating with Others*

THE POWER OF CREATIVITY AND INNOVATION

Creativity and innovation refer to the ability to generate new and unique ideas and develop them into valuable products, services, or processes. They are powerful tools that can help organizations to:

- *Solve problems*

Creativity and innovation can be used to find new and effective solutions to problems that might otherwise be difficult to solve.

- *Increase efficiency*

By continuously looking for new and better ways to do things, organizations can improve their efficiency and reduce costs.

- *Increase competitiveness*

By developing new products and services, organizations can differentiate themselves from their competitors and gain a competitive advantage.

- *Drive growth*

Innovation can lead to new revenue streams and opportunities for growth.

- ***Foster a positive work environment***

Encouraging creativity and innovation can help to foster a positive work environment by giving employees a sense of purpose and the opportunity to contribute to the organization's success.

- ***Meet customer needs***

Innovation can help organizations to understand customer needs and develop products, services, or processes that meet those needs.

- ***Stay relevant***

Continuously innovating can help organizations to stay relevant and adapt to changing market conditions.

- ***Create new opportunities***

Innovation can create new opportunities for an organization, whether it's a new product, a new market, or a new business model.

- ***Enhance learning***

Creativity and innovation can enhance learning by encouraging experimentation and exploration.

- ***Build resilience***

Innovation can help organizations to build resilience by encouraging them to be adaptable and to find new opportunities in changing circumstances.

IMPROVING CREATIVE SKILLS

Creative skills refer to the ability to generate new and unique ideas and to develop them into valuable products, services, or processes. Examples of creative skills include:

- ***Idea generation***

The ability to come up with new and unique ideas.

- ***Problem-solving***

The ability to find new and effective solutions to problems.

- ***Innovation***

The ability to take ideas and develop them into something new and valuable.

- ***Divergent thinking***

The ability to come up with many different ideas, rather than just one.

- ***Convergent thinking***

The ability to take many different ideas and combine them into one solution.

- ***Visualization***

The ability to create mental images of what something might look like.

- *Intuition*

The ability to trust one's instincts and to be open to new ideas.

- *Flexibility*

The ability to adapt to new situations and to be open to change.

- *Imagination*

The ability to see beyond what currently exists and to envision new possibilities.

To improve your creative skills, there are several things you can do:

1. Dedicating Time for Creativity

Dedicating time to creativity can improve creative skills by providing an opportunity to focus on generating new and original ideas, as well as developing existing skills and techniques. It can also help to overcome creative blocks and stimulate new and unique ideas.

Dedicating time for creativity can be done in a variety of ways, such as setting aside time each day or week to work on a specific project, or taking a break from work or other responsibilities to engage in a creative pursuit. This can help to create a sense of discipline and routine, which can be beneficial for the creative process.

An example of this is the famous author, Stephen King, who writes for at least four hours every morning, no matter what, He has a strict routine to write a certain amount of words every day, and this discipline allows him to finish a book in a few months. By dedicating time to creativity, King can produce a large body of work, including novels, short stories, and essays, that have been widely acclaimed and have become best sellers. Another example is the artist Yayoi Kusama, who dedicates several hours every day to her art practice. Through her dedicated time to creativity, Kusama has been able to develop a unique and recognizable style and has become one of the most successful and influential artists of her time. Her works are known for their repetitive patterns and vibrant colors and have been exhibited in galleries and museums around the world.

2. *Keeping an Idea Journal*

Keeping an idea journal can improve creative skills by providing a tool for capturing and organizing ideas, and by allowing one to reflect on their progress and progress over time. It allows one to record and save ideas as they come and revisit them later. For example, a product designer who wants to improve their creative skills might keep an idea journal where they record sketches and notes about different product concepts. They could also use the journal to record observations about consumer behavior and user needs. By keeping an idea journal, the designer can easily refer back to previous ideas and see how their skills have developed over time.

Additionally, keeping an idea journal can help to increase productivity, as it allows one to have a record of previous ideas and to have them readily available for future reference. It also allows one to reflect on their progress and to identify areas that need improvement. It also allows one to think outside of the box and explore new ways of thinking, which can lead to more effective solutions and decision-making.

3. Broadening your Perspective

Broadening your perspective can improve your creative skills by exposing you to new and diverse ways of thinking, which can lead to more original and innovative ideas. This can be done by actively seeking out and engaging with different cultures, perspectives, and experiences.

For example, a designer who primarily works with Western aesthetics might benefit from studying and incorporating elements of Eastern design, such as Japanese minimalism or traditional Chinese patterns. This can lead to a more unique and diverse body of work, as well as a deeper understanding and appreciation of different cultures and design styles.

An example of this can be seen in the works of fashion designer, Vivienne Westwood, who drew inspiration from punk culture, political activism, and traditional British tailoring to create a unique and diverse body of work that still resonates today.

4. Taking Inspiration from Diverse Sources

Taking inspiration from diverse sources can improve creative skills by exposing one to a wide range of ideas, perspectives, and techniques. This can help to break out of creative ruts and stimulate new and unique ideas. For example, an artist who typically draws inspiration from traditional art forms such as painting and sculpture might begin to incorporate elements from street art, digital art, or even science and technology into their work, leading to a more diverse and dynamic body of work. This can be seen in the works of artists like the street artist Banksy, who incorporate elements of political satire and social commentary into their work, or contemporary artist Ai Weiwei draws inspiration from Chinese history and culture, as well as global politics and human rights.

5. Practicing Brainstorming Techniques

Practicing brainstorming techniques can improve creative skills by providing a structured method for generating new and original ideas. Brainstorming can be done individually or in a group setting, and often involves generating as many ideas as possible in a set period without judging or evaluating them. This can help to overcome creative blocks and stimulate new and unique ideas.

One example of a brainstorming technique is called "random word" where you take a word and associate it with a problem you are trying to solve. For example, if you are a company trying to come up with new marketing ideas, you might take the word "butterfly" and brainstorm different ways it could be used in a marketing campaign, such as creating a butterfly-themed product line or using butterfly imagery in advertising. This technique can be a fun and effective way to generate new and original ideas.

Another example is "SCAMPER" which is an acronym for Substitute, Combine, Adapt, Modify, Put to another use, Eliminate, and Reverse. This technique can be used to take an existing idea or product and come up with new and innovative ways to use it. For example, an artist might use this technique to come up with new and unique ways to use a specific medium or material in their work.

6. *Playing with different Mediums and Techniques*

Playing with different mediums and techniques can improve creative skills by exposing you to new ways of creating and expressing yourself. Experimenting with different mediums and techniques can help to break out of creative ruts and stimulate new and unique ideas. It can also help to develop new skills and techniques and expand your understanding of the creative process.

For example, a painter who typically works with oils might benefit from experimenting with watercolors or mixed media, as each medium has its unique properties and techniques. This can lead to a more diverse and dynamic body of work, as well as a deeper understanding of the medium and the creative process. An example of this can be seen in the works of Salvador Dali, who incorporated various mediums and techniques in his artwork, such as painting, sculpture, film, and photography. He used techniques like the 'paranoid-critical method' and 'hand-painted dream photographs' which allowed him to create unique and surreal artworks. Through experimenting with different mediums and techniques, Dali was able to develop a unique and recognizable style that continues to be highly influential in the art world.

7. *Collaborating with Others*

Collaborating with others can improve creative skills by exposing you to new perspectives, ideas, and techniques. It can also help to overcome creative blocks and stimulate new and unique ideas. Collaboration can also help to build teamwork, communication, and leadership skills.

Working with other people on a creative project can also help to push the boundaries of what is possible and challenge you to think differently, which can ultimately lead to more innovative and original ideas.

An example of this can be seen in the music industry where many songs are written by multiple songwriters. For example, the song "Uptown Funk" by Mark Ronson and Bruno Mars, collaborated to create a unique and catchy song that blended elements of funk, soul, and pop music. Through their collaboration, Ronson and Mars were able to create a hit song that resonated with audiences around the world and earned multiple awards and accolades.

Another example is the design firm IDEO, which brings together multi-disciplinary teams of designers, engineers, anthropologists, and other experts to collaborate on projects and come up with innovative solutions. This approach has led to the development of products such as the first computer mouse for Apple and the first portable blood glucose meter for diabetics. The collaboration allowed for diverse and unique ideas to come together and create something truly innovative.

Financial Management and Planning

Overview

- ❖ *Introduction*
- ❖ *Improving Financial Management Skills*
  - ✓ *Setting Clear Financial Goals and Objectives*
  - ✓ *Developing a Comprehensive Budget*
  - ✓ *Forecasting Future Financial Performance*
  - ✓ *Implementing Financial Controls and Monitoring Systems*
  - ✓ *Regularly Reviewing and Analyzing Financial Data*
  - ✓ *Seeking Professional Financial Advice*
  - ✓ *Continuously Improving Financial Planning and Management Procedures*
  - ✓ *Building a Strong Financial Team*
  - ✓ *Staying Updated on Market Conditions*
  - ✓ *Building and Maintaining a Robust Financial Information System*
  - ✓ *Implementing Risk Management Strategies*

INTRODUCTION

Financial management and planning refer to the process of managing an organization's financial resources to achieve its objectives. This includes developing and implementing financial strategies, creating and managing budgets, forecasting future financial performance, and making decisions about investments and other financial matters.

A key aspect of financial management is the creation of a budget, which is a detailed plan for how an organization will allocate its financial resources over a certain period. This typically includes projected income and expenses, as well as plans for any investments or other financial transactions.

Forecasting future financial performance is another important aspect of financial management. This involves using historical financial data, as well as information about external factors such as the economy and industry trends, to make predictions about how an organization's financial performance is likely to change in the future. This information can then be used to make decisions about investments, expansion plans, and other financial matters.

Another important aspect of financial management is investment management. This involves making decisions about how to allocate the organization's financial resources to achieve the best possible returns. This can include decisions about which stocks or bonds to buy, as well as decisions about real estate investments, venture capital, and other types of investments.

Overall, financial management and planning are crucial aspects of running a successful organization, as they allow leaders to make informed decisions about how to allocate resources and navigate the often-complex financial landscape.

Let's understand this with two examples:

1. A small retail business wants to open a second location. As part of their financial management and planning, the business owner conducts a thorough analysis of the potential costs and revenues associated with opening a new store. This includes forecasting projected sales, estimating the costs of leasing a new space, hiring new employees, and buying inventory, as well as considering external factors such as the local economy and competition in the area. Using this information, the business owner creates a detailed budget for the new store and develops a plan for how to finance the expansion, including options such as taking out a loan or seeking out investors.

2. A non-profit organization that provides services to the homeless wants to expand its services to a new city. As part of its financial management and planning, the organization conducts a cost-benefit analysis to determine the feasibility of expanding to a new location. This includes forecasting projected costs such as rent for a new

facility, salaries for new employees, and operational expenses, as well as estimating potential revenue from donations, grants, and government funding. The organization also conducts market research to learn about the demand for their services in the new city, the competition, and the funding resources available in the new location. Based on the analysis, the organization creates a detailed budget and fundraising plan for the expansion and secures funding from a combination of government grants and private donations.

IMPROVING FINANCIAL MANAGEMENT SKILLS

Effective financial management is important for the success of any organization or business. Here are some ways to improve financial management:

1. Setting Clear Financial Goals and Objectives

Setting clear financial goals and objectives can improve financial management by providing a roadmap for making informed and strategic financial decisions. It can also help to prioritize spending and saving and to measure progress toward achieving financial goals.

Clear financial goals and objectives should be specific, measurable, achievable, relevant, and time-bound

(SMART). For example, a specific financial goal could be to save $20,000 for a down payment on a house within the next two years. This goal is specific, measurable (the amount saved), achievable (with a budget and savings plan), relevant (to the individual's desire to purchase a house), and time-bound (within the next two years).

When a person has a clear financial goal, it becomes easier to make informed decisions on how to allocate their resources. They can prioritize spending and saving based on what will help them reach their goal, and evaluate the effectiveness of their financial decisions by measuring progress towards achieving their goal.

An example of this is a person who has a goal of saving for retirement. They set a specific goal to save a certain amount by a certain age and make a plan to increase their savings rate, reduce their expenses, and invest in appropriate vehicles. This person can make better financial decisions in the present, such as cutting back on unnecessary expenses, to reach their long-term goal of being financially secure in retirement.

2. *Developing a Comprehensive Budget*

Developing a comprehensive budget can improve financial management by providing a clear picture of income and expenses, and by highlighting areas where adjustments can be made to achieve financial goals. A budget is a financial plan that helps to track and control the flow of money, and it is an essential tool for managing finances.

The Triumphant Mind – Success Rituals

A comprehensive budget should include all sources of income, as well as all regular and expected expenses. This includes fixed expenses such as rent or mortgage, utility bills, and insurance, as well as variable expenses such as groceries, entertainment, and transportation. By tracking all of these expenses, it becomes possible to identify areas where cost-cutting is possible, or where more money could be allocated toward savings or other financial goals.

An example of this is a person who is trying to pay off credit card debt. By creating a comprehensive budget, this person can identify how much money is going towards credit card payments, and how much is left over for other expenses. With this information, the person can make adjustments, such as cutting back on discretionary spending and redirecting that money toward paying off the debt. Additionally, the person can also look at ways to increase income, such as taking on a part-time job, to help pay off the debt faster.

In conclusion, a comprehensive budget is an essential tool for improving financial management. It helps to track and control the flow of money, identify areas where adjustments can be made, and achieve financial goals.

3. *Forecasting Future Financial Performance*

Forecasting future financial performance can improve financial management by providing insight into potential future financial scenarios and allowing for proactive planning and decision-making. It allows individuals, businesses, and organizations to anticipate and prepare for potential financial challenges, and make necessary adjustments to achieve financial goals.

Forecasting future financial performance can be done using various techniques such as trend analysis, financial modeling, and scenario planning. This process involves analyzing historical financial data and using it to predict future financial performance. It helps to identify potential risks, opportunities, and trends that may impact financial performance.

For example, a business owner who regularly forecasts their financial performance can identify potential future challenges such as a decline in sales or an increase in operating costs. This information can be used to make strategic decisions such as cutting costs, diversifying products or services, or seeking additional funding. By preparing for potential challenges in advance, the business owner is better positioned to weather unexpected financial downturns and achieve their financial goals.

In conclusion, forecasting future financial performance is an important aspect of financial management. It allows individuals, businesses, and organizations to anticipate and prepare for potential financial challenges, and make necessary adjustments to achieve financial goals. This is done by analyzing historical financial data and using it to predict future financial performance, which can help to identify potential risks, opportunities, and trends that may impact financial performance.

4. Implementing Financial Controls and Monitoring Systems

Implementing financial controls and monitoring systems can improve financial management by providing a framework for ensuring accuracy, integrity, and accountability in financial transactions. These controls and systems can help to prevent errors and fraud, and ensure compliance with laws and regulations. They also help to detect any financial irregularities and allow for timely corrective action to be taken.

Examples of financial controls and monitoring systems include internal controls, such as segregation of duties, which can help to prevent fraud by ensuring that no one person has complete control over a financial transaction, and regular financial audits, which can help to identify errors and irregularities. Other examples include setting up a system to record and track financial transactions and implementing procedures for reconciling accounts.

An example of a company that has implemented financial controls and monitoring systems is Walmart. The company has an internal audit team that conducts regular audits of the financial records and operations to ensure compliance with laws and regulations, as well as to identify any errors or fraud. Additionally, Walmart has implemented an internal control system that includes segregation of duties and regular financial reporting to senior management. These financial controls and monitoring systems have helped to ensure the accuracy and integrity of the company's financial records and have helped to prevent fraud and errors.

In conclusion, implementing financial controls and monitoring systems is an important aspect of financial management. It provides a framework for ensuring accuracy, integrity, and accountability in financial transactions, and helps to prevent errors and fraud while ensuring compliance with laws and regulations. This allows for timely corrective action to be taken when irregularities are detected and improve the overall financial management of an organization.

5. *Regularly Reviewing and Analyzing Financial Data*

Regularly reviewing and analyzing financial data can improve financial management by providing insight into the financial health and performance of an individual, business, or organization. It can help to identify trends, patterns, and areas for improvement, and help make more informed financial decisions.

Reviewing and analyzing financial data can be done by analyzing financial statements such as balance sheets, income statements, and cash flow statements. These statements provide information on the financial performance of an individual, business, or organization over a while, such as revenue, expenses, assets, liabilities, and cash flow. By reviewing and analyzing this data regularly, it is possible to identify trends, patterns, and areas for improvement, such as cost savings opportunities, areas of inefficiency, or potential risks. An example of a company that regularly reviews and analyzes financial data is Amazon. The company regularly analyzes financial data such as revenue, expenses, and customer data to identify trends and patterns.

This information is used to make informed decisions about the direction of the business, such as expanding into new markets or investing in new technologies. Additionally, Amazon also regularly reviews and analyzes customer data to identify trends in customer behavior and preferences, which are used to improve the company's products and services.

In conclusion, regularly reviewing and analyzing financial data is an essential aspect of financial management. It provides insight into the financial health and performance of an individual, business, or organization, and helps to identify trends, patterns, and areas for improvement. This allows for more informed financial decisions that can ultimately improve the overall financial management of an organization.

6. Seeking Professional Financial Advice

Seeking professional financial advice can improve financial management by providing expertise and guidance on a wide range of financial matters, such as investment, tax planning, retirement planning, and estate planning. Professional financial advisors can help individuals and businesses to make informed decisions about their finances, and develop a comprehensive financial plan that aligns with those goals and objectives.

Professional financial advisors can also provide valuable insights into market conditions, emerging trends, and investment opportunities, which can be especially helpful for businesses. They also keep up-to-date with changes in laws and regulations, which can be especially important for businesses and individuals who operate in specialized fields.

An example of this is a business owner who seeks the advice of a financial advisor to help them develop a comprehensive financial plan for their business. The advisor can help the business owner to identify their goals, assess their current financial situation, and develop a plan to achieve their goals. This may include advice on investment strategies, tax planning, risk management, and cash flow management. Additionally, the advisor can also provide valuable insights into market conditions, emerging trends, and investment opportunities, which can help the business owner to make informed decisions about the future of their business.

In conclusion, seeking professional financial advice can improve financial management by providing expertise and guidance on a wide range of financial matters. Professional financial advisors can help individuals and businesses to make informed decisions about their finances, and develop a comprehensive financial plan that aligns with their goals and objectives. They also provide valuable insights into market conditions, emerging trends, and investment opportunities, which can be especially helpful for businesses.

7. Continuously Improving Financial Planning and Management Procedures

Continuously improving financial planning and management procedures can improve financial management by ensuring that an individual, business, or organization is operating at peak efficiency and effectively achieving its financial goals. This can be done by regularly reviewing and updating financial plans and procedures, identifying areas for improvement, and implementing changes as needed. For example, a business might regularly review its financial statements and compare them to industry benchmarks to identify areas where it is underperforming. Based on this analysis, the business might decide to implement new financial management procedures, such as cost-cutting measures or changes to its pricing strategy.

An example of a company that continuously improves its financial planning and management procedures is Google.

The company has a reputation for being financially savvy, and it regularly reviews and updates its financial plans and procedures. For example, Google has implemented a data-driven approach to budgeting and forecasting, which allows it to make informed decisions about its spending and investments. Additionally, Google also regularly reviews its financial performance and compares it to industry benchmarks to identify areas where it can improve its financial management procedures. Through this continuous improvement process, Google has been able to maintain a strong financial position and achieve its financial goals.

In conclusion, continuously improving financial planning and management procedures can improve financial management by ensuring that an individual, business, or organization is operating at peak efficiency and effectively achieving its financial goals. This can be done by regularly reviewing and updating financial plans and procedures, identifying areas for improvement, and implementing changes as needed. This process allows an organization to adapt to changes in the market, and make informed decisions that can lead to long-term financial stability.

8. *Building a Strong Financial Team*

Building a strong financial team can improve financial management by providing expertise, knowledge, and support in various financial areas such as accounting, budgeting, and financial analysis. A strong financial team can help to ensure that financial information is accurate, complete, and timely and that financial goals are met. The team can also help to identify and mitigate financial risks and provide valuable insights and advice on financial decisions.

For example, a business might have a team that includes a financial manager, an accountant, and a financial analyst. The financial manager is responsible for the overall financial management of the business and developing financial strategies. The accountant is responsible for maintaining accurate financial records and ensuring compliance with tax laws and regulations. The financial analyst is responsible for analyzing financial data and identifying trends that can inform the decision-making process.

An example of a company that has built a strong financial team is Berkshire Hathaway. The company is led by Warren Buffet, who is considered one of the most successful investors in the world. A buffet is supported by a team of financial experts, including Charlie Munger, who serves as

Vice Chairman, and several investment managers, who are responsible for analyzing and selecting investments. Through the expertise and knowledge of this team, Berkshire Hathaway has been able to achieve long-term financial success and has become one of the most successful and profitable companies in the world.

9. Staying Updated on Market Conditions

Staying updated on market conditions can improve financial management by providing insight into economic trends and market fluctuations, which can inform financial decisions. This can include monitoring economic indicators, such as interest rates, inflation, and gross domestic product (GDP), as well as keeping up to date with developments in specific industries and markets. By staying informed about market conditions, individuals, businesses, and organizations can make more informed financial decisions and adapt to changes in the market.

An example of a company that stays updated on market conditions is JPMorgan Chase, one of the largest banks in the world. The bank has a team of economists and market analysts who monitor economic indicators and market fluctuations on a global scale. This information is used to inform the bank's investment decisions, as well as its lending and risk management policies. Additionally, JPMorgan Chase also stays updated on developments in specific industries, such as technology and healthcare, to identify potential opportunities for growth and expansion.

For an individual, staying updated on market conditions can mean reading business news, following trends in the stock market, and keeping an eye on interest rates and the economy. By staying informed about the economy and the stock market, an individual can make more informed decisions about their investments and savings.

In conclusion, staying updated on market conditions can improve financial management by providing insight into economic trends and market fluctuations, which can inform financial decisions.

This can include monitoring economic indicators, such as interest rates, inflation, and gross domestic product (GDP), as well as keeping up to date with developments in specific industries and markets. By staying informed about market conditions, individuals, businesses, and organizations can make more informed financial decisions and adapt to changes in the market.

10. Building and Maintaining a Robust Financial Information System

Building and maintaining a robust financial information system can improve financial management by providing accurate, reliable, and timely financial information that can be used to make informed financial decisions. A robust financial information system can include various tools and technologies such as accounting software, financial analysis software, and data visualization tools. These systems can be used to automate financial processes, such as invoicing, budgeting, and financial reporting. They also provide the ability to store and access financial data and provide real-time insights into financial performance.

An example of a company that has built and maintains a robust financial information system is Amazon. The company has a sophisticated financial information system that includes a variety of tools and technologies such as accounting software, financial analysis software, and data visualization tools. This system is used to automate financial processes such as invoicing, budgeting, and financial reporting, and provides real-time insights into financial performance. Additionally, the system also enables Amazon to store and access financial data, which is used to make informed financial decisions, such as pricing strategies and investment decisions.

For an individual, building and maintaining a robust financial information system can be achieved by keeping accurate records of income and expenses, and having a budget in place. Additionally, individuals can use financial management software or apps to keep track of their financial information and monitor their financial performance.

In conclusion, building and maintaining a robust financial information system can improve financial management by providing accurate, reliable, and timely financial information that can be used to make informed financial decisions. A robust financial information system can include various tools and technologies such as accounting software, financial analysis software, and data visualization tools. These systems can be used to automate financial processes, store and access financial data, and provide real-time insights into financial performance.

11. Implementing Risk Management Strategies

Implementing risk management strategies can improve financial management by identifying and mitigating potential financial risks that could negatively impact an individual, business, or organization. Risk management strategies include identifying potential risks, assessing their likelihood and potential impact, and implementing measures to mitigate or manage those risks. By implementing risk management strategies, an individual, business or organization can minimize the impact of unexpected events and make more informed financial decisions.

An example of a company that has implemented risk

management strategies is Apple. The company has implemented a risk management strategy that includes identifying potential risks, such as a downturn in the economy or a shift in consumer preferences, assessing the likelihood and potential impact of those risks, and implementing measures to mitigate or manage them. For example, Apple diversifies its product line and has a strong cash reserve to mitigate the impact of a downturn in the economy.

Additionally, Apple continuously monitors market trends and customer preferences to adapt to changes and stay ahead of the competition.

For an individual, implementing risk management strategies can include diversifying investments, having an emergency fund, and having insurance. By diversifying investments, an individual can minimize the impact of a downturn in a specific market or industry. Having an emergency fund can help an individual to manage unexpected expenses, and having insurance can protect an individual from financial losses due to unforeseen events.

In conclusion, implementing risk management strategies can improve financial management by identifying and mitigating potential financial risks that could negatively impact an individual, business, or organization. Risk management strategies include identifying potential risks, assessing their likelihood and potential impact, and implementing measures to mitigate or manage those risks. By implementing risk management strategies, an individual, business or organization can minimize the impact of unexpected events and make more informed financial decisions.

Self-discipline and Self-control

Overview

- ❖ *Introduction*
- ❖ *Importance of Self-discipline and Self-control*
  - ✓ *Staying Focused and Avoiding Distractions*
  - ✓ *Managing Emotions and Impulses*
  - ✓ *Overcoming Procrastination*
  - ✓ *Maintaining a Positive Mindset*
  - ✓ *Managing Stress and Pressure*
  - ✓ *Building Resilience*
  - ✓ *Making Sound Decisions*
  - ✓ *Maintaining Self-motivation*
  - ✓ *Building and Maintaining Healthy Habits*
  - ✓ *Improving Interpersonal Relationships*
  - ✓ *Managing Finances and Budgets Effectively*

INTRODUCTION

Self-discipline and self-control refer to the ability to control one's thoughts, emotions, and actions to achieve a desired outcome or goal.

- Self-discipline: Self-discipline is the ability to set and follow through on goals, even when faced with distractions or temptations. It involves the ability to prioritize and stay focused on what is important, even in the face of adversity. For example, a professional athlete may need to have the self-discipline to stick to a strict training regimen and avoid distractions such as parties or too much TV.

- Self-control: Self-control is the ability to resist the urge to do something that may be harmful or counterproductive to achieve a desired outcome. It involves the ability to manage impulses and regulate behavior to achieve a goal. For example, a student may need to have the self-control to resist the temptation to procrastinate and stay focused on studying for an exam.

Some other examples are:

- An entrepreneur who has self-discipline will be able to stay focused on the long-term goals of the business and prioritize work even when faced with distractions such as social media notifications.

- A person who wants to lose weight will have to have the self-control to resist the temptation of eating high-calorie foods and to stick to a healthy diet plan.

IMPORTANCE OF SELF-DISCIPLINE AND SELF-CONTROL

Self-discipline and self-control are important for personal and professional development. They can help individuals to achieve their goals and to lead a more fulfilling life. Several reasons can explain the importance of self-discipline and self-control. The following are:

1. Staying Focused and Avoiding Distractions

Staying focused and avoiding distractions is important for achieving self-discipline and self-control because it allows an individual to direct their attention and energy towards a specific task or goal. Distractions can divert attention and energy away from the task at hand, making it more difficult to maintain focus and achieve the desired outcome.

Self-discipline and self-control are essential for achieving goals and making progress in various areas of life, such as career, finances, health, and personal development. By staying focused and avoiding distractions, an individual can develop the ability to control their impulses and resist temptations that may impede their progress.

An example of this is an individual who wants to improve their fitness level. The individual sets a goal to exercise regularly but finds it difficult to maintain focus and stay on track due to distractions such as social media, television, and other activities. By staying focused and avoiding distractions, the individual can direct their attention and energy toward their goal of exercising regularly and achieving their desired outcome.

In conclusion, staying focused and avoiding distractions is important for achieving self-discipline and self-control because it allows an individual to direct their attention and energy towards a specific task or goal. Distractions can divert attention and energy away from the task at hand, making it more difficult to maintain focus and achieve the desired outcome. Self-discipline and self-control are essential for achieving goals and making progress in various areas of life, such as career, finances, health, and personal development. By staying focused and avoiding distractions, an individual can develop the ability to control their impulses and resist temptations that may impede their progress.

2. *Managing Emotions and Impulses*

Managing emotions and impulses is important for achieving self-discipline and self-control because it allows an individual to make rational decisions, rather than acting on emotions or impulses. Emotions and impulses can cloud judgment and cause an individual to make impulsive or short-sighted decisions that may not align with their long-term goals.

Self-discipline and self-control are essential for achieving goals and making progress in various areas of life, such as career, finances, health, and personal development. By managing emotions and impulses, an individual can develop the ability to control their reactions and responses to situations, and make thoughtful, well-considered decisions that align with their goals and values.

An example of this is an individual who wants to improve their finances. The individual sets a goal to save money but finds it difficult to resist the impulse to spend money on unnecessary items. By managing emotions and impulses, the individual can control their reactions and responses to the impulse to spend money, and make thoughtful, well-considered decisions that align with their goal of saving money.

In conclusion, managing emotions and impulses is important for achieving self-discipline and self-control because it allows an individual to make rational decisions, rather than acting on emotions or impulses. Emotions and impulses can cloud judgment and cause an individual to make impulsive or short-sighted decisions that may not align with their long-term goals.

By managing emotions and impulses, an individual can develop the ability to control their reactions and responses to situations, and make thoughtful, well considered decisions that align with their goals and values.

3. Overcoming Procrastination

Overcoming procrastination is important for achieving self-discipline and self-control because it allows an individual to take action toward their goals and responsibilities. Procrastination can create a cycle of delay and inactivity, making it difficult to achieve desired outcomes and meet deadlines.

Self-discipline and self-control are essential for achieving goals and making progress in various areas of life, such as career, finances, health, and personal development. By overcoming procrastination, an individual can develop the ability to take action toward their goals and responsibilities, rather than delaying or avoiding them.

An example of this is an individual who wants to improve their career. The individual sets a goal to complete a certification but finds it difficult to start studying due to procrastination. By overcoming procrastination, the individual can take action towards their goal of completing the certification and make progress towards their desired outcome.

In conclusion, overcoming procrastination is important for achieving self-discipline and self-control because it allows an individual to take action toward their goals and responsibilities. Procrastination can create a cycle of delay and inactivity, making it difficult to achieve desired outcomes and meet deadlines. By overcoming procrastination, an individual can develop the ability to take action toward their goals and responsibilities, rather than delaying or avoiding them. This allows for a more proactive approach toward achieving goals and making progress in various areas of life.

4. Maintaining a Positive Mindset

Maintaining a positive mindset is important for achieving self-discipline and self-control because it allows an individual to approach challenges and obstacles with a sense of optimism and determination. A positive mindset can foster resilience and perseverance in the face of adversity and can help an individual to stay motivated and focused on their goals.

Self-discipline and self-control are essential for achieving goals and making progress in various areas of life, such as career, finances, health, and personal development. By maintaining a positive mindset, an individual can develop the ability to overcome obstacles and setbacks, and stay motivated and focused on achieving their goals.

An example of this is an individual who wants to improve their physical fitness. The individual sets a goal to run a marathon but finds it difficult to stay motivated and focused due to a lack of progress. By maintaining a positive mindset, the individual can approach the challenge with optimism and determination, and stay motivated and focused on their goal of running a marathon.

In conclusion, maintaining a positive mindset is

important for achieving self-discipline and self-control because it allows an individual to approach challenges and obstacles with a sense of optimism and determination. A positive mindset can foster resilience and perseverance in the face of adversity and can help an individual to stay motivated and focused on their goals. Self-discipline and self-control are essential for achieving goals and making progress in various areas of life, such as career, finances, health, and personal development. By maintaining a positive mindset, an individual can develop the ability to overcome obstacles and setbacks, and stay motivated and focused on achieving their goals.

5. *Managing Stress and Pressure*

Managing stress and pressure is important for achieving self-discipline and self-control because it allows an individual to maintain a clear and focused mind, even in challenging or stressful situations. Stress and pressure can negatively impact an individual's mental and physical well-being, making it difficult to maintain focus and control over thoughts and actions.

Self-discipline and self-control are essential for achieving goals and making progress in various areas of life, such as career, finances, health, and personal development. By managing stress and pressure, an individual can develop the ability to remain calm and focused under pressure, and make rational decisions.

An example of this is an individual who has an important

presentation to give in front of a large audience. The individual finds it hard to manage the stress and pressure of the situation. By managing stress and pressure, individuals can learn to remain calm, focus on the task at hand, and present their ideas clearly and effectively.

In conclusion, managing stress and pressure is important for achieving self-discipline and self-control because it allows an individual to maintain a clear and focused mind, even in challenging or stressful situations. Stress and pressure can negatively impact an individual's mental and physical well-being, making it difficult to maintain focus and control over thoughts and actions. By managing stress and pressure, an individual can develop the ability to remain calm and focused under pressure, and make rational decisions. This is vital for achieving goals and making progress in various areas of life, such as career, finances, health, and personal development.

6. Building Resilience

Building resilience is important for achieving self-discipline and self-control because it allows an individual to bounce back from difficult situations and adversity, and maintain a positive attitude and perspective. Resilience enables an individual to better handle stress and pressure and to maintain focus and self-control in the face of challenges or setbacks.

Self-discipline and self-control are essential for achieving goals and making progress in various areas of life, such as career, finances, health, and personal development. By building resilience, an individual can develop the ability to handle difficult situations and setbacks and to maintain motivation and focus on achieving their goals.

An example of this is an individual who wants to start their own business. The individual faces multiple setbacks, such as a lack of funding and difficulty in finding the right team. By building resilience, the individual can bounce back from these setbacks and maintain a positive attitude, and continue to work towards their goal of starting their own business.

In conclusion, building resilience is important for achieving self-discipline and self-control because it allows an individual to bounce back from difficult situations and adversity, and maintain a positive attitude and perspective. Resilience enables an individual to better handle stress and pressure and to maintain focus and self-control in the face of challenges or setbacks. By building resilience, an individual can develop the ability to handle difficult situations and setbacks and to maintain motivation and focus on achieving their goals. This is vital for achieving progress in various areas of life, such as career, finances, health, and personal development.

7. *Making Sound Decisions*

Making sound decisions is important for achieving self-discipline and self-control because it allows an individual to make rational and well-considered choices that align with their goals and values. It enables an individual to control their impulses, resist temptations, and make choices that align with their long-term goals, rather than short-term impulses or desires.

Self-discipline and self-control are essential for achieving goals and making progress in various areas of life, such as career, finances, health, and personal development. By making sound decisions, an individual can develop the ability to control their impulses, resist temptations, and make choices that align with their long-term goals.

An example of this is an individual who wants to improve their finances. The individual sets a goal to save money but finds it difficult to resist the impulse to spend money on unnecessary items. By making sound decisions, individuals can control their impulses, resist temptations, and make choices that align with their goal of saving money.

In conclusion, making sound decisions is important for achieving self-discipline and self-control because it allows an individual to make rational and well considered choices that align with their goals and values. It enables an individual to control their impulses, resist temptations, and make choices that align with their long-term goals, rather than short-term impulses or desires. Self-discipline and self-control are essential for achieving goals and making progress in various areas of life, such as career, finances, health, and personal development. By making sound decisions, an individual can develop the ability to control their impulses, resist temptations, and make choices that align with their long-term goals.

8. *Maintaining Self-motivation*

Maintaining self-motivation is important for achieving self-discipline and self-control because it allows an individual to stay focused and engaged in their goals and to persevere through challenging situations. Without self-motivation, it can be difficult to maintain the discipline and control needed to achieve long-term goals.

Self-discipline and self-control are essential for achieving goals and making progress in various areas of life, such as career, finances, health, and personal development. By maintaining self-motivation, an individual can develop the ability to stay focused and engaged in their goals and to persevere through challenging situations. An example of this is an individual who wants to learn a new language. The individual sets a goal to become fluent in the language but finds it difficult to stay motivated and focused due to the difficulty of the task. By maintaining self-motivation, the individual can stay focused and engaged in their goal, and persevere through the challenges of learning a new language.

In conclusion, maintaining self-motivation is important for achieving self-discipline and self-control because it allows an individual to stay focused and engaged in their goals and to persevere through challenging situations. Without self-motivation, it can be difficult to maintain the discipline and control needed to achieve long-term goals. By maintaining self-motivation, an individual can develop the ability to stay focused and engaged in their goals and to persevere through challenging situations.

This is vital for achieving progress in various areas of life, such as career, finances, health, and personal development.

9. *Building and Maintaining Healthy Habits*

Building and maintaining healthy habits is important for achieving self-discipline and self-control because it allows an individual to establish a routine and structure in their daily life, which in turn makes it easier to maintain focus and control over thoughts and actions. Healthy habits promote self-discipline and self-control by promoting physical and mental well-being, which can improve overall performance in various areas of life.

Self-discipline and self-control are essential for achieving goals and making progress in various areas of life, such as career, finances, health, and personal development. By building and maintaining healthy habits, an individual can develop the ability to establish a routine and structure in their daily life, making it easier to maintain focus and control over thoughts and actions.

An example of this is an individual who wants to improve their physical health. The individual sets a goal to exercise regularly and eat a healthy diet. By building and maintaining healthy habits such as exercising for 30 minutes every day and planning healthy meals, the individual can establish a routine and structure in their daily life that promotes self-discipline and self-control, making it easier to achieve their goal of improving their physical health.

In conclusion, building and maintaining healthy habits is important for achieving self-discipline and self-control because it allows an individual to establish a routine and structure in their daily life, which in turn makes it easier to maintain focus and control over thoughts and actions. Healthy habits promote self-discipline and self-control by promoting physical and mental well-being, which can improve overall performance in various areas of life. By building and maintaining healthy habits, an individual can develop the ability to establish a routine and structure in their daily life, making it easier to maintain focus and control over thoughts and actions. This is vital for achieving progress in various areas of life, such as career, finances, health, and personal development.

10. Improving Interpersonal Relationships

Improving interpersonal relationships is important for achieving self-discipline and self-control because it allows an individual to develop effective communication and social skills, which can help them to navigate and manage the various relationships and interactions in their life. Good interpersonal relationships can provide support, guidance, and accountability, which can help an individual to maintain self-discipline and self-control.

Self-discipline and self-control are essential for achieving goals and making progress in various areas of life, such as career, finances, health, and personal development. By improving interpersonal relationships, an individual can develop the ability to effectively communicate and navigate social interactions, which can help them to maintain self-discipline and self-control.

An example of this is an individual who wants to improve their work-life balance. The individual sets a goal to disconnect from work-related activities during non-working hours but finds it difficult to disconnect. By improving their interpersonal relationships, such as setting boundaries with colleagues and managers, the individual can effectively communicate and navigate social interactions, which can help them to maintain self-discipline and self-control by disconnecting from work-related activities during non-working hours.

In conclusion, improving interpersonal relationships is important for achieving self-discipline and self-control because it allows an individual to develop effectively communication and social skills, which can help them to navigate and manage the various relationships and interactions in their life. Good interpersonal relationships can provide support, guidance, and accountability, which can help an individual to maintain self-discipline and self-control. By improving interpersonal relationships, an individual can develop the ability to effectively communicate and navigate social interactions, which can help them to maintain self-discipline and self-control, and achieve progress in various areas of life, such as career, finances, health, and personal development.

11. Managing Finances and Budgets Effectively

Managing finances and budgets effectively is important for achieving self-discipline and self-control because it allows an individual to make well-informed and rational decisions about their money, and to prioritize their spending in line with their goals and values. By creating and sticking to a budget, an individual can develop self-discipline in managing their finances and avoid impulse spending, which can lead to financial problems.

Self-discipline and self-control are essential for achieving goals and making progress in various areas of life, such as career, finances, health, and personal development. By managing finances and budgets effectively, an individual can develop the ability to make well-informed and rational decisions about their money and to prioritize their spending in line with their goals and values. An example of this is an individual who wants to save money for a down payment on a house. The individual sets a budget that allocates their income towards savings, living expenses, and other necessary expenses. By managing their finances and budgets effectively, individuals can prioritize their spending and allocate their income towards saving for a down payment, which will help them to achieve their goal of buying a house.

In conclusion, Managing finances and budgets effectively is important for achieving self-discipline and self-control because it allows an individual to make well-informed and rational decisions about their money, and to prioritize their spending in line with their goals and values. By creating and sticking to a budget, an individual can develop self-discipline in managing their finances and avoid impulse spending, which can lead to financial problems. This can help an individual to achieve progress in various areas of life, such as career, finances, health, and personal development.

12. Improving Self-discipline and Self-control

Improving self-discipline and self-control is important for achieving self-discipline and self-control because it allows an individual to develop the ability to control their thoughts, emotions, and actions, which in turn makes it easier to maintain focus and control over their behavior. The more self-discipline and self-control an individual has, the better they will be able to resist temptations, manage stress, and pressure, and achieve their goals.

Self-discipline and self-control are essential for achieving goals and making progress in various areas of life, such as career, finances, health, and personal development. By improving self-discipline and self-control, an individual can develop the ability to control their thoughts, emotions, and actions, which in turn makes it easier to maintain focus and control over their behavior.

An example of this is an individual who wants to quit smoking. The individual sets a goal to quit smoking but finds it difficult to resist the urge to smoke. By improving self-discipline and self-control, the individual can develop the ability to control their thoughts, emotions, and actions, which in turn makes it easier to maintain focus and control over their behavior. This will help the individual to resist the urge to smoke, and achieve their goal of quitting smoking.

In conclusion, Improving self-discipline and self-control is important for achieving self-discipline and self-control because it allows an individual to develop the ability to control their thoughts, emotions, and actions, which in turn makes it easier to maintain focus and control over their behavior. The more self-discipline and self-control an individual has, the better they will be able to resist temptations, manage stress and pressure, and achieve their goals. This can help an individual to achieve progress in various areas of life, such as career, finances, health, and personal development.

Resilience and Adaptability

Overview

- ❖ *Introduction*
- ❖ *Improving Resilience and Adaptability*
    - ✓ *Embracing Change*
    - ✓ *Taking Calculated Risks*
    - ✓ *Remaining Calm under Pressure*
    - ✓ *Continuously Learning*
    - ✓ *Building and Maintaining a Positive Attitude*
    - ✓ *Building a Support Network*
    - ✓ *Being Flexible and Open-minded*
    - ✓ *Developing Effective Problem-solving Skills*
    - ✓ *Seeking out New Challenges and Opportunities*
    - ✓ *Building and Maintaining a Diverse Set of Skills*
    - ✓ *Being Self-aware*
    - ✓ *Being Proactive and Taking Initiatives*

INTRODUCTION

Resilience refers to the ability to cope with and adapt to challenging situations, and to bounce back from setbacks and adversity. It is the psychological and emotional ability to withstand stress, pressure, and uncertainty and to maintain a positive outlook and well-being.

Resilience is significant because it enables individuals and organizations to navigate through difficult times, recover from setbacks and maintain a sense of well-being, and move forward positively.

- *Personal resilience*

Resilience can help individuals to cope with personal challenges such as relationship problems, health issues, or financial difficulties. For example, a person who has experienced a significant loss, such as the death of a loved one, may demonstrate resilience by finding ways to cope with their grief and to move forward with their life.

- *Organizational resilience*

Resilience can also be important for organizations to navigate through difficult times such as economic downturns, natural disasters, or pandemics. For example, an organization that has a culture of resilience may be better able to adapt to changes in the market, or to recover quickly from a crisis, than one that lacks resilience.

Some other examples may include:

- A soldier who is deployed to a combat zone may demonstrate resilience by being able to adapt to the stress and uncertainty of war and maintain a positive outlook.

- A company that experiences a natural disaster, such as a flood or a fire, may demonstrate resilience by quickly bouncing back and getting back to normal operations as quickly as possible.

IMPROVING RESILIENCE AND ADAPTABILITY

Resilience and adaptability are important skills that can be developed and strengthened. Here are some ways to improve resilience and adaptability:

1. Embracing Change

Embracing change can improve resilience and adaptability by enabling individuals to approach new and unfamiliar situations with a sense of curiosity and openness, rather than fear and resistance. When individuals can embrace change, they are more likely to be able to adapt to new circumstances and find new opportunities for growth and development. Furthermore, embracing change can help individuals to develop a sense of flexibility and to become more open to new ideas and perspectives.

For example, imagine a business owner who is faced

with the challenge of a rapidly changing market. If they can embrace change, they may be more likely to view this challenge as an opportunity to innovate and find new ways to grow their business. They may be more open to experimenting with new business models and products, and to seek out new opportunities.

Additionally, by embracing change, the business owner may be more likely to stay current and relevant in their field, and to be able to adapt to future changes more easily. On the other hand, if the business owner resists change and holds on to outdated methods and ideas, they may struggle to adapt and compete in the rapidly changing market.

2. Taking Calculated Risks

Taking calculated risks can improve resilience and adaptability by challenging individuals to step out of their comfort zones and try new things. This can help them develop new skills, perspectives, and ways of thinking.

For example, an individual who is considering starting their own business may take a calculated risk by leaving their current job and investing their savings into their new venture. This risk can be considered calculated because the individual has done thorough market research, created a business plan, and has a clear understanding of the potential rewards and potential downsides. This calculated risk can lead to personal and professional growth, increased confidence, and potentially a successful business.

3. Remaining Calm under Pressure

Remaining calm under pressure can improve resilience and adaptability by allowing individuals to think clearly and make rational decisions in difficult situations. When faced with stress, it's easy to become overwhelmed and make impulsive decisions, but maintaining a sense of calm allows one to evaluate the situation objectively, and make a well-thought-out decision.

An example of this would be an emergency room doctor who remains calm under pressure while treating a patient in critical condition. By staying calm and focused, they can make quick and accurate decisions, which can ultimately save the patient's life.

In this example, the doctor's ability to remain calm under pressure not only improves the outcome for the patient but also contributes to the doctor's resilience and adaptability, as they can handle high-stress situations effectively.

4. Continuously Learning

Continuously learning can improve resilience and adaptability by expanding one's knowledge, skills, and abilities, and by keeping up with changes in one's field. This allows individuals to be better equipped to handle new challenges and adapt to changing circumstances.

For example, an IT professional who continuously learns new technologies and programming languages will be a better equipped to handle new projects and adapt to changing industry trends. This person will have more experience and knowledge, which will make them more valuable to their employer and also more attractive to potential employers. Additionally, continuous learning will also make them more resilient as they will be less likely to be caught off-guard by changes and new challenges in their field.

5. Building and Maintaining a Positive Attitude

A positive attitude can improve resilience and adaptability by helping individuals to view challenges and obstacles as opportunities for growth and learning. When an individual has a positive attitude, they are more likely to approach difficult situations with a sense of optimism and determination, rather than feeling defeated or overwhelmed. This can enable them to more easily adapt to change and bounce back from setbacks.

For example, imagine an employee who is faced with a difficult task at work, such as a last-minute project with a tight deadline. If the employee has a positive attitude, they may approach the task with enthusiasm and a sense of determination, viewing it as an opportunity to showcase their skills and capabilities. They may also be more open to feedback and suggestions from others, which can help them to find creative solutions and complete the task successfully. On the other hand, if the employee has a negative attitude, they may view the task as a burden and be more likely to feel stressed and overwhelmed, which can make it more difficult for them to adapt and complete the task.

6. Building a Support Network

Building a support network can improve resilience and adaptability by providing individuals with a sense of connection and belonging, as well as the emotional and practical support they need to navigate difficult situations. Having a network of friends, family members, and colleagues who care about them can help individuals to feel less alone and more capable of handling challenges. Additionally, having a support network can provide a sounding board for ideas, help with problem-solving, and give an individual a different perspective on a problem.

For example, imagine an individual who has recently experienced a major life change, such as a divorce or a job loss. If they have a strong support network, they may be better able to cope with the emotional and practical challenges that come with this change. They may be able to lean on friends and family members for emotional support and guidance, and may also be able to rely on their network for practical assistance, such as help with childcare or job searching. Additionally, the network can provide the individual with a sense of belonging and connection, which can help them to feel more resilient and adaptable in the face of change. On the other hand, if the individual lacks a support network, they may feel isolated and overwhelmed, which can make it more difficult for them to cope with and adapt to the change.

7. *Being Flexible and Open-minded*

Being flexible and open-minded can improve resilience and adaptability by enabling individuals to approach situations with a sense of curiosity and a willingness to try new things.

When an individual is open-minded and flexible, they are more likely to be able to adapt to new and unexpected circumstances and to find innovative solutions to problems. Additionally, being open to change and new ideas can help individuals to stay current and relevant in their field.

For example, imagine an entrepreneur who is faced with a rapidly changing market. If entrepreneur is flexible and open-minded, they may be able to adapt to the changing market by experimenting with new business models or products, and by seeking out new opportunities. They may also be more likely to be open to feedback and new ideas from employees, partners, and customers, which can help them to stay competitive and find new ways to grow their business. On the other hand, if the entrepreneur is inflexible and closed-minded, they may be more likely to resist change and stick with outdated methods and ideas, which can make it more difficult for them to adapt and succeed in a rapidly changing market.

8. Developing Effective Problem-solving Skills

Developing effective problem-solving skills can improve resilience and adaptability by enabling individuals to identify and analyze problems, and find creative and effective solutions. When individuals can develop problem-solving skills, they are more likely to approach challenges with a sense of confidence and determination, rather than feeling defeated or overwhelmed. Additionally, effective problem-solving skills can help individuals to identify and mitigate potential risks, and plan for future challenges.

For example, imagine an engineer who is tasked with designing a new product. If the engineer has developed effective problem-solving skills, they may be able to identify and analyze the challenges and constraints of the project, and to develop creative and effective solutions. They may also be able to identify potential risks and challenges and plan for them, which can help to ensure the success of the project. On the other hand, if the engineer lacks effective problem-solving skills, they may be more likely to feel overwhelmed and defeated by the challenges of the project and may struggle to find effective solutions.

9. Seeking out New Challenges and Opportunities

Seeking out new challenges and opportunities can improve resilience and adaptability by encouraging individuals to step out of their comfort zones and take on new and unfamiliar tasks. When individuals are exposed to new experiences and situations, they are more likely to develop new skills and learn from their mistakes. Additionally, taking on new challenges can help individuals to build confidence in their abilities and to develop a growth mindset, which is the belief that abilities and intelligence can be developed. For example, imagine a student who is considering a career in a field they have never studied before. If they seek out new challenges and opportunities in that field, such as internships or volunteer work, they will be exposed to new experiences, people, and skills that can help them to develop new perspectives, learn new skills, and build confidence in their abilities. Additionally, by taking on new challenges, they can develop a growth mindset and learn to persevere in the face of setbacks and difficulties. On the other hand, if student avoids new challenges and sticks to what they already know, they may miss out on valuable learning opportunities and may struggle to adapt to new and unfamiliar situations in the future.

10. Building and Maintaining a Diverse Set of Skills

Building and maintaining a diverse set of skills can improve resilience and adaptability by enabling individuals to approach challenges and opportunities from multiple perspectives and with a variety of tools and techniques. When individuals have a diverse set of skills, they are more likely to be able to adapt to changing circumstances and find creative solutions to problems. Additionally, having a diverse set of skills can also make an individual more valuable and versatile in their field, as they will be able to tackle a wider range of tasks and projects.

For example, imagine an artist who primarily works in painting, but also has experience in sculpture, graphic design, and photography. If they have a diverse set of skills, they will be able to adapt to changing art trends and will be able to apply the techniques they have learned in one medium to another. Additionally, having a diverse set of skills can open up new opportunities for the artist, such as being able to take on graphic design projects or creating installations that integrate various art forms. On the other hand, if the artist only has experience in one medium, they may struggle to adapt to changing trends and find new opportunities for growth and development.

11. Being Self-aware

Being self-aware can improve resilience and adaptability by enabling individuals to understand their strengths, weaknesses, values, and emotions. When individuals are self-aware, they are better able to understand how their thoughts, feelings, and behaviors are impacting their ability to adapt to change and handle challenges.

Additionally, self-awareness also helps individuals to understand their limitations and to set realistic goals for themselves. With self-awareness, individuals can develop an understanding of their own needs and can learn to manage their emotions, thoughts, and behaviors more effectively.

For example, imagine an individual who is going through a difficult time in their personal life, such as a breakup or a family issue. If they are self-aware, they will be better able to understand how their thoughts and emotions are impacting their ability to cope with the situation. They may be able to identify negative thought patterns, such as rumination, and take steps to change them. Additionally, they may be able to take a step back and reflect on their own needs and how they can best take care of themselves during this time. On the other hand, if the individual is not self-aware, they may struggle to understand the impact of their thoughts and emotions on their ability to cope with the situation and may not be able to manage their emotions, thoughts, and behaviors effectively.

12. Being Proactive and Taking Initiatives

Being proactive and taking initiative can improve resilience and adaptability by empowering individuals to take control of their own lives and shape their futures. When individuals are proactive, they are more likely to identify and pursue opportunities, take initiative in finding solutions to problems, and create a sense of purpose and direction. Additionally, by taking initiative, individuals learn to be resourceful, find ways to overcome obstacles, and develop a sense of self-efficacy, the belief that they can make things happen.

For example, imagine an employee who is dissatisfied with their current job, but wants to change it. If they are proactive and take initiative, they will be more likely to research and identify new job opportunities, network and make contacts, and take steps to improve their skills and qualifications. They may also be more likely to take the initiative to speak to their manager about their dissatisfaction and to find ways to improve their current job situation. Additionally, by taking initiative, the employee will be better able to shape their career path and create a sense of purpose and direction. On the other hand, if the employee is not proactive and does not take initiative, they may be more likely to feel stuck in their current job and struggle to find new opportunities for growth and development.

Emotional Intelligence and Stress Management

Overview

- ❖ Introduction
- ❖ Achieving Emotional Intelligence
  - ✓ Self-awareness
  - ✓ Self-regulation
  - ✓ Motivation
  - ✓ Empathy
  - ✓ Social skills
  - ✓ Understanding and Managing Emotions
  - ✓ Building Positive Relationships
  - ✓ Communicating Effectively
  - ✓ Dealing with Stress and Pressure
  - ✓ Conflict Resolution
  - ✓ Building and Maintaining Emotional Resilience
  - ✓ Reflecting on Personal Biases and Prejudices
  - ✓ Growing Emotionally
- ❖ Improving Stress Management
  - ✓ Identifying and Eliminating the Sources of Stress
  - ✓ Developing Effective Coping Strategies
  - ✓ Building a Support Group
  - ✓ Maintaining a Healthy Lifestyle
  - ✓ Prioritizing Self-care

- *Learning to Say No*
- *Practicing Mindfulness and Relaxation Techniques*
- *Setting Boundaries*
- *Managing Time and Setting Realistic Goals*
- *Building and Maintaining a Positive Mindset*
- *Seeking Professional Help when Necessary*
- *Building and Maintaining a Work-life Balance*
- *Maintaining Emotional Resilience*

INTRODUCTION

Emotional intelligence (EI) refers to the ability to recognize, understand, and manage one's own emotions, as well as the emotions of others. It involves several components such as self-awareness, self-regulation, motivation, empathy, and social skills, list goes on....

Examples:

- A salesperson who has high emotional intelligence may be able to read the emotions of potential clients and adapt their sales pitch to better connect with them.

- A teacher who has high emotional intelligence may be able to empathize with students from diverse backgrounds and create a positive and inclusive learning environment.

- A therapist who has high emotional intelligence may be able to understand the emotions of their clients and help them healthily process their feelings.

- A leader who has high emotional intelligence may be able to recognize and manage their own emotions and create a positive and productive work environment for their team.

- A customer service representative who has high emotional intelligence may be able to manage difficult or angry customers with empathy and understanding, defusing potential conflicts and maintaining positive relationships.

- A manager who has high emotional intelligence may be able to recognize when their team members are feeling stressed or overwhelmed, and take steps to help them manage their emotions and improve their work performance.

ACHIEVING EMOTIONAL INTELLIGENCE

Emotional intelligence can be developed and strengthened through practice and effort. Here are some ways to achieve emotional intelligence:

1. Self-awareness

Self-awareness is the ability to recognize and understand one's own emotions, thoughts, and behaviors. It is the foundation of emotional intelligence, as it allows an individual to manage their own emotions and respond to the emotions of others constructively.

For example, a self-aware individual may recognize that they are feeling stressed and overwhelmed. They can then take steps to manage their stress, such as taking a break or practicing relaxation techniques, rather than lashing out at others or becoming disengaged. Additionally, because they are aware of their own emotions, they may be better able to understand and empathize with the emotions of others.

2. Self-regulation

Self-regulation is the ability to manage one's own emotions, thoughts, and behaviors to achieve one's goals and maintain emotional well-being. It is an essential aspect of emotional intelligence, as it allows an individual to effectively respond to their own emotions and the emotions of others.

For example, an individual with strong self-regulation skills may be able to calm themselves down when they are feeling angry or frustrated, rather than reacting impulsively or aggressively. They may also be able to set and achieve goals despite setbacks or obstacles because they can regulate their emotions and stay motivated.

Additionally, self-regulation can also help an individual to manage their impulses, think before acting, and to manage stress, which can help them to be more effective in relationships, work, and life in general.

3. Motivation

Motivation is the driving force behind an individual's actions and behaviors. It is an important aspect of emotional intelligence, as it allows an individual to set and achieve goals, and to maintain a positive attitude and outlook in the face of challenges and setbacks.

For example, an individual who is highly motivated to achieve a specific goal, such as getting a promotion or starting a business, may be better able to regulate their emotions and stay focused despite obstacles or setbacks. They may also be more likely to be persistent and resilient in the face of challenges because they are motivated to achieve their goal. Additionally, motivated individuals may be more likely to maintain positive relationships, because they are driven to succeed and may inspire others to do the same.

In general, motivation can help individuals to achieve their goals, and to manage their emotions, thoughts, and behaviors in a way that helps them to be more effective in their personal and professional lives.

4. *Empathy*

Empathy is the ability to understand and share the feelings of others. It is a key component of emotional intelligence, as it allows an individual to respond to the emotions of others in a compassionate and understanding way.

For example, an empathetic individual may be able to sense when a colleague or friend is going through a difficult time and offer support and understanding. They may also be able to work effectively in a team because they can understand and value the perspectives and emotions of other team members.

Additionally, empathy can also help individuals to build stronger relationships and to communicate effectively because they can understand the feelings, thoughts, and needs of others, and respond in a way that is appropriate and effective. Moreover, empathy can help to reduce conflicts and to create a positive and supportive environment, which can foster creativity, productivity, and collaboration. In summary, empathy is a crucial aspect of emotional intelligence, as it allows individuals to connect with others, communicate effectively, and build strong and positive relationships.

5. *Social skills*

Social skills refer to the ability to effectively interact and communicate with others, as well as to build and maintain positive relationships. They are an important aspect of emotional intelligence, as they allow an individual to navigate social situations, understand and respond appropriately to the emotions of others, and maintain positive relationships.

For example, an individual with strong social skills may be able to effectively negotiate a difficult conversation or conflict with a coworker, because they can understand the other person's perspective and communicate effectively. They may also be able to build strong and positive relationships with colleagues, friends, and family members because they can effectively communicate and understand the emotions of others.

Additionally, social skills can also help individuals to be more effective in the workplace, in their personal and professional relationships, and other social settings. Because they can understand and respond to the emotions of others, they can be better leaders, better collaborators, and better at building trust and creating positive and supportive environments. In summary, social skills are an essential aspect of emotional intelligence, as they allow individuals to navigate social situations, communicate effectively and build positive relationships with others.

6. Understanding and Managing Emotions

Understanding and managing emotions is the ability to recognize and understand one's own emotions, as well as the emotions of others, and to respond to them constructively and effectively. It is an essential aspect of emotional intelligence, as it allows an individual to navigate and navigate complex social situations, communicate effectively, and build and maintain positive relationships.

For example, an individual who understands and manages their emotions well may be able to recognize when they are feeling stressed or overwhelmed and take steps to manage their stress, such as taking a break or practicing relaxation techniques, rather than lashing out at others or becoming disengaged. They may also be able to understand and empathize with the emotions of others, which can help them to communicate effectively and build stronger relationships.

Additionally, understanding and managing emotions can also help individuals to be more effective in the workplace, in their personal and professional relationships, and other social settings. Because they can understand and respond to their own emotions and the emotions of others, they can be better leaders, better collaborators, and better at building trust and creating positive and supportive environments. In summary, understanding and managing emotions is an essential aspect of emotional intelligence, as it allows individuals to navigate social situations, communicate effectively and build positive relationships with others.

7. *Building Positive Relationships*

Building positive relationships is the ability to connect with others, establish trust, and maintain positive interactions and communication. It is an essential aspect of emotional intelligence, as it allows an individual to navigate social situations, understand and respond to the emotions of others, and maintain positive relationships.

For example, an individual who can build positive relationships may be able to work effectively in a team, because they can understand and value the perspectives and emotions of other team members. They may also be able to build strong and positive relationships with colleagues, friends, and family members because they can effectively communicate and understand the emotions of others.

Additionally, building positive relationships can also help individuals to be more effective in the workplace, in their personal and professional relationships, and other social settings. Because they can connect with others, establish trust, and maintain positive interactions and communication, they can be better leaders, better collaborators, and better at creating positive and supportive environments.

In summary, building positive relationships is an essential aspect of emotional intelligence, as it allows individuals to connect with others, establish trust, and maintain positive interactions and communication, which can help them to be more effective in their personal and professional lives.

8. *Communicating Effectively*

Communicating effectively refers to the ability to convey information clearly, actively listen and understand the perspective of others, and respond appropriately to their emotions and needs. It is an essential aspect of emotional intelligence, as it allows an individual to navigate social situations, understand and respond to the emotions of others, and maintain positive relationships.

For example, an individual who can communicate effectively may be able to negotiate a difficult conversation or conflict with a coworker or friend, because they can understand the other person's perspective and convey their thoughts and feelings clearly and calmly. They may also be able to build stronger relationships because they can communicate and understand the emotions of others. Additionally, communicating effectively can also help individuals to be more effective in the workplace, in their personal and professional relationships, and other social settings.

Because they can convey information clearly, actively listen, and respond appropriately to the emotions of others, they can be better leaders, better collaborators, and better at building trust and creating positive and supportive environments. In summary, communicating effectively is an essential aspect of emotional intelligence, as it allows individuals to navigate social situations, understand and respond to the emotions of others, and maintain positive relationships.

9. *Dealing with Stress and Pressure*

Dealing with stress and pressure refers to the ability to manage emotions and behaviors when faced with challenging and potentially overwhelming situations. It is an important aspect of emotional intelligence, as it allows an individual to stay calm, focused, and effective in the face of stress and pressure.

For example, an individual who can effectively deal with stress and pressure may be able to stay calm and focused during a high-pressure meeting or presentation, because they can manage their own emotions and stay on task. They may also be able to bounce back quickly from setbacks or disappointments because they can healthily manage their emotions and maintain a positive outlook.

Additionally, dealing with stress and pressure can also help individuals to be more effective in the workplace, in their personal and professional relationships, and other social settings. Because they can healthily manage their emotions and behaviors, they can be better leaders, better collaborators, and better at creating positive and supportive environments.

In summary, dealing with stress and pressure is an important aspect of emotional intelligence, as it allows individuals to manage their emotions and behaviors in a healthy way, which can help them to be more effective in their personal and professional lives.

10. Conflict Resolution

Conflict resolution refers to the ability to manage and resolve disputes and disagreements constructively and effectively. It is an important aspect of emotional intelligence, as it allows an individual to navigate and navigate complex social situations, understand and respond appropriately to the emotions of others, and maintain positive relationships.

For example, an individual who is skilled in conflict resolution may be able to successfully negotiate and resolve a dispute with a coworker or family member, because they can understand the perspectives and emotions of all parties involved and find a solution that is acceptable to everyone. They may also be able to build stronger relationships because they can manage conflicts positively and constructively.

Additionally, conflict resolution can also help individuals to be more effective in the workplace, in their personal and professional relationships, and other social settings. Because they can manage and resolve disputes and disagreements constructively and effectively, they can be better leaders, better collaborators, and better at creating positive and supportive environments.

In summary, conflict resolution is an essential aspect of emotional intelligence, as it allows individuals to navigate complex social situations, understand and respond appropriately to the emotions of others, and maintain positive relationships.

11. Building and Maintaining Emotional Resilience

Building and maintaining emotional resilience refers to the ability to bounce back from difficult situations and to maintain emotional well-being in the face of stress and adversity. It is an important aspect of emotional intelligence, as it allows an individual to manage their own emotions and respond to the emotions of others constructively.

For example, an individual who has developed emotional resilience may be able to handle a difficult situation, such as a job loss or a personal setback, without becoming overwhelmed or disengaged. They may be able to maintain a positive outlook and find new opportunities because they can manage their emotions and stay motivated.

Additionally, emotional resilience can also help individuals to be more effective in the workplace, in their personal and professional relationships, and other social settings. Because they can handle stress and adversity well, they can be better leaders, better collaborators, and better at creating positive and supportive environments.

In summary, building and maintaining emotional resilience is an important aspect of emotional intelligence, as it allows individuals to manage their own emotions and respond to the emotions of others in a constructive way, which can help them to be more effective in their personal and professional lives.

12. Reflecting on Personal Biases and Prejudices

Reflecting on personal biases and prejudices refers to the ability to recognize and understand one's preconceptions and stereotypes, and to actively work to overcome them. It is an important aspect of emotional intelligence, as it allows an individual to navigate and navigate complex social situations, understand and respond appropriately to the emotions of others, and maintain positive relationships.

For example, an individual who reflects on their personal biases and prejudices may be able to better understand and relate to people from different backgrounds, cultures, and experiences, because they can recognize and overcome their preconceptions and stereotypes. They may also be more effective in a diverse work environment because they can understand and value the perspectives and emotions of people from different backgrounds.

Additionally, reflecting on personal biases and prejudices can also help individuals to be more effective in the workplace, in their personal and professional relationships, and other social settings. Because they can understand and respond appropriately to the emotions of others, they can be better leaders, better collaborators, and better at creating positive and supportive environments.

In summary, reflecting on personal biases and prejudices is an important aspect of emotional intelligence, as it allows individuals to understand and respond appropriately to the emotions of others, and to maintain positive relationships in a diverse and complex social environment.

13. Growing Emotionally

Growing emotionally refers to the ability to develop and improve one's emotional intelligence over time. It is an ongoing process that involves self-awareness, self-regulation, motivation, empathy, social skills, understanding, and managing emotions, building positive relationships, communicating effectively, dealing with stress and pressure, conflict resolution, building and maintaining emotional resilience, and reflecting on personal biases and prejudices.

For example, an individual who is committed to growing emotionally may actively seek out new learning and development opportunities, such as workshops, coaching, mentoring, or therapy. They may also practice mindfulness or other techniques that help them to better understand and manage their emotions. Through this process, they may become more self-aware, more empathetic, and better able to communicate and build positive relationships, and better at dealing with stress and pressure.

Additionally, growing emotionally can also help individuals to be more effective in the workplace, in their personal and professional relationships, and other social settings. Because they are continuously developing and improving their emotional intelligence, they can be better leaders, better collaborators, and better at creating positive and supportive environments.

In summary, growing emotionally is an ongoing process that allows individuals to develop and improve their emotional intelligence over time, which can help them to be more effective in their personal and professional lives.

IMPROVING STRESS MANAGEMENT

Stress management is the process of identifying, assessing, and reducing stress in one's life. It involves developing coping strategies and techniques to manage the physical and emotional effects of stress.

Stress management can help individuals to improve their overall well-being and to perform better in their personal and professional lives.

Here are some examples of the importance of stress management:

- A busy professional might use stress management techniques such as time management and relaxation techniques to help them to stay focused and productive in their job, despite the high-pressure demands of their work.
- A person who is dealing with a chronic illness might use stress management techniques such as relaxation techniques, to help them to manage the emotional and physical symptoms of their condition, and to improve their overall well-being.

Now, let's see some ways that are effective for Improving Stress Management:

1. Identifying and Eliminating the Sources of Stress

Identifying and eliminating the sources of stress is an important step in improving stress management. By identifying the specific things that are causing stress, an individual can take action to remove or reduce them. This can help to reduce overall stress levels and prevent the negative effects of chronic stress on mental and physical health.

For example, an individual who is experiencing stress at work may identify that a heavy workload and unrealistic deadlines are the main sources of stress. They may then

The Triumphant Mind – Success Rituals

take action to address these sources of stress by speaking to their manager about their workload or looking for ways to manage their time more efficiently. This may involve delegating some tasks, setting more realistic deadlines, or prioritizing the most important tasks. By taking these steps, the individual can reduce their stress levels and improve their overall well-being.

Additionally, identifying and eliminating sources of stress can also help individuals to be more effective in the workplace, in their personal and professional relationships, and other social settings. Because they can manage their stress levels, they can be more productive, more creative, and more resilient, which can help them to be more effective in their personal and professional lives.

In summary, identifying and eliminating sources of stress is an important step in improving stress management, as it allows individuals to take action to reduce or remove the things that are causing stress, which can help them to be more effective in their personal and professional lives.

2. Developing Effective Coping Strategies

Developing effective coping strategies is an important step in improving stress management. Coping strategies are specific techniques or actions that an individual can use to manage stress, such as relaxation techniques, physical exercise, time management, or seeking social support. By developing a range of effective coping strategies, an individual can be better equipped to manage stress when it arises.

For example, an individual who is experiencing stress may develop a coping strategy of regularly engaging in physical exercises, such as going for a run or taking a yoga class. This can help to reduce stress by releasing endorphins and improving overall physical and mental well-being. They may also develop a coping strategy of regularly practicing mindfulness or meditation, which can help them to stay calm, focused, and centered in the face of stress.

Additionally, developing effective coping strategies can also help individuals to be more effective in the workplace, in their personal and professional relationships, and other social settings. Because they can manage their stress levels, they can be more productive, more creative, and more resilient, which can help them to be more effective in their personal and professional lives.

In summary, developing effective coping strategies is an important step in improving stress management, as it allows individuals to have a set of tools and techniques that they can use to manage stress when it arises, which can help them to be more effective in their personal and professional lives.

3. *Building a Support Group*

Building a support group can help improve stress management by providing individuals with a network of people who can offer emotional and practical support during times of stress. A support group can consist of friends, family members, or professionals, who can offer a listening ear, a shoulder to lean on, or practical advice and assistance.

For example, an individual who is experiencing stress may build a support group of friends and family members with whom they can talk about their stress and receive emotional support. They may also seek out a support group of people who are going through similar experiences, such as a support group for people who are dealing with a chronic illness or for people who have lost a loved one. In this way, they can share their experiences, get emotional support and gain practical insights on how

to cope with stress.

Additionally, building a support group can also help individuals to be more effective in the workplace, in their personal and professional relationships, and other social settings. Because they have a network of people they can turn to for support, they can be more resilient, better at dealing with stress, and more effective in their personal and professional lives.

In summary, building a support group can help improve stress management by providing individuals with a network of people who can offer emotional and practical support during times of stress, which can help them to be more effective in their personal and professional lives.

4. *Maintaining a Healthy Lifestyle*

Maintaining a healthy lifestyle can help improve stress management by providing individuals with the physical and mental resources they need to manage stress. This can include things like regular exercise, a healthy diet, adequate sleep, and avoiding alcohol, tobacco, and other drugs.

For example, an individual who is experiencing stress may maintain a healthy lifestyle by engaging in regular exercise such as going for a run or taking a yoga class. This can help reduce stress by releasing endorphins and improving overall physical and mental well-being. They may also maintain a healthy diet and get enough sleep, which can help to improve overall energy and focus and reduce the negative effects of stress on the body. Additionally, they may avoid alcohol, tobacco, and other drugs, which can exacerbate stress and negatively impact physical and mental health.

Additionally, maintaining a healthy lifestyle can also help individuals to be more effective in the workplace, in their personal and professional relationships, and other social settings. Because they have the physical and mental resources to manage stress, they can be more productive, more creative, and more resilient, which can help them to be more effective in their personal and professional lives.

In summary, maintaining a healthy lifestyle can help improve stress management by providing individuals with the physical and mental resources they need to manage stress, which can help them to be more effective in their personal and professional lives.

5. Prioritizing Self-care

Prioritizing self-care can help improve stress management by helping individuals to take care of their physical, emotional, and mental well-being. It is an essential aspect of stress management as it helps individuals to replenish their physical and emotional resources, which are depleted by stress.

For example, an individual who is experiencing stress may prioritize self-care by taking regular breaks throughout the day to rest, relax and recharge. They may also engage in activities that they enjoy such as reading, listening to music, or spending time with friends and family. Additionally, they may make sure to get enough sleep, eat well, and exercise regularly.

By prioritizing self-care, the individual is better equipped to handle stress and maintain a balance in their life. Additionally, prioritizing self-care can also help individuals to be more effective in the workplace, in their personal and professional relationships, and other social settings. Because they take care of themselves and replenish their physical and emotional resources, they can be more productive, more creative, and more resilient which can help them to be more effective in their personal and professional lives.

In summary, prioritizing self-care can help improve

stress management by helping individuals to take care of their physical, emotional, and mental well-being, which can help them to be more effective in their personal and professional lives.

6. Practicing Mindfulness and Relaxation Techniques

Practicing mindfulness and relaxation techniques can help improve stress management by helping individuals to focus on the present moment, reduce anxiety and tension, and to improve overall well-being. Mindfulness techniques such as meditation, deep breathing exercises, and yoga, can help individuals to become more aware of their thoughts and emotions, and to detach from them in a non-judgmental way. Relaxation techniques such as progressive muscle relaxation, visualization, and guided imagery, can help individuals to reduce tension and anxiety and to promote relaxation.

For example, an individual who is experiencing stress may practice mindfulness techniques such as meditation before going to bed, this can help them to let go of the day's stressors and fall asleep faster. They may also practice relaxation techniques such as progressive muscle relaxation during their lunch break, this can help them to reduce tension and anxiety and to improve their overall well-being during the workday.

Additionally, practicing mindfulness and relaxation techniques can also help individuals to be more effective in the workplace, in their personal and professional relationships, and other social settings. Because they can manage their stress levels, they can be more productive, more creative, and more resilient, which can help them to be more effective in their personal and professional lives.

In summary, practicing mindfulness and relaxation techniques can help improve stress management by helping individuals to focus on the present moment, reduce anxiety and tension, and improve overall well-being, which can help them to be more effective in their personal and professional lives.

7. Setting Boundaries

Setting boundaries can help improve stress management by helping individuals to establish and maintain clear limits with others regarding their time, energy, and resources. When individuals set boundaries, they are communicating their needs and limits, and are making it clear what they are willing and able to do. This can help to reduce the amount of stress and emotional demands that they experience, as they are not overcommitted or overextending themselves.

For example, an individual who is experiencing stress from work may set boundaries with their colleagues or boss by clearly communicating their availability and capacity for work, this can help to reduce the number of unrealistic expectations and demands that they experience. They may also set boundaries with their friends and family by clearly communicating their availability and capacity for socializing and leisure activities, this can help to reduce the amount of stress and emotional demands that they experience from their personal life.

Additionally, setting boundaries can also help individuals to be more effective in the workplace, in their personal and professional relationships, and other social settings. Because they can manage their time, energy, and resources, they can be more productive, more creative, and more resilient, which can help them to be more effective in their personal and professional lives.

In summary, setting boundaries can help improve stress management by helping individuals to establish and maintain clear limits with others concerning their time, energy, and resources, which can help them to be more effective in their personal and professional lives.

8. *Learning to Say "No"*

Learning to say "no" can help improve stress management by helping individuals to establish and maintain clear limits with others, and to better manage their time, energy, and resources. Saying "no" allows individuals to set boundaries and prioritize their own needs and well-being. It can help them to avoid overcommitting and overextending themselves, which can lead to increased stress and burnout.

For example, an individual who is experiencing stress from work may learn to say "no" to taking on additional responsibilities or projects that are not essential to their job role. This can help them to focus on their current responsibilities and to manage their workload more effectively. They may also learn to say "no" to social invitations that they are not comfortable with or that would interfere with their time and well-being.

Additionally, learning to say "no" can also help individuals to be more effective in the workplace, in their personal and professional relationships, and other social settings. Because they can manage their time, energy, and resources, and they can be more productive, more creative, and more resilient, which can help them to be more effective in their personal and professional lives.

In summary, learning to say "no" can help improve stress management by helping individuals to establish and maintain clear limits with others, and to better manage their time, energy, and resources, which can help them to be more effective in their personal and professional lives.

9. *Managing Time and Setting Realistic Goals*

Managing time and setting realistic goals can help improve stress management by helping individuals to prioritize their tasks, to focus on what is important, and to avoid feeling overwhelmed. When individuals set realistic goals, they can break down larger tasks into smaller, manageable chunks, and work on them one at a time. This can help to reduce the amount of stress and anxiety that they experience, as they are not trying to accomplish too much at once.

For example, an individual who is experiencing stress from work may set realistic goals by breaking down a large project into smaller tasks and prioritizing them. They may also manage their time by creating a schedule that allows them to focus on one task at a time and avoid multitasking, which can increase stress and decrease productivity. Additionally, they may also set realistic deadlines for themselves and communicate them with their team or manager, this can help to keep the project on track and avoid last-minute rushes and unrealistic expectations.

Additionally, managing time and setting realistic goals can also help individuals to be more effective in the workplace, in their personal and professional relationships, and other social settings. Because they can manage their time and set realistic goals, they can be more productive, more creative, and more resilient, which can help them to be more effective in their personal and professional lives.

In summary, managing time and setting realistic goals can help improve stress management by helping individuals to prioritize their tasks, to focus on what is important, and to avoid feeling overwhelmed, which can help them to be more effective in their personal and professional lives.

10. Building and Maintaining a Positive Mindset

Building and maintaining a positive mindset can help improve stress management by helping individuals to view challenges and stressors more positively and constructively. A positive mindset can help individuals to focus on solutions rather than problems, maintain a sense of perspective, and develop a sense of resilience and optimism.

For example, an individual who is experiencing stress may build and maintain a positive mindset by focusing on the things that are going well in their life and by practicing gratitude. They may also use positive affirmations, visualization, and other cognitive techniques to reframe negative thoughts and emotions. Additionally, they may also engage in activities that bring them joy and positivity, such as spending time in nature, practicing a hobby, or listening to music.

Additionally, building and maintaining a positive mindset can also help individuals to be more effective in the workplace, in their personal and professional relationships, and other social settings. Because they have a positive outlook, they can be more productive, more creative, and more resilient, which can help them to be more effective in their personal and professional lives.

In summary, building and maintaining a positive mindset can help improve stress management by helping individuals to view challenges and stressors more positively and constructively, which can help them to be more effective in their personal and professional lives.

11. Seeking Professional Help when Necessary

Seeking professional help when necessary can help improve stress management by providing individuals with access to specialized knowledge, skills, and resources that can help them to better understand and manage their stress. Professional help can include therapy, counseling, or medication.

For example, an individual who is experiencing severe or prolonged stress may seek professional help from a therapist or counselor. They can work together to identify the causes of stress, develop coping strategies and techniques, and provide emotional support. Additionally, a therapist can also help the individual to explore any underlying mental health concerns that may be contributing to their stress.

Additionally, seeking professional help can also help individuals to be more effective in the workplace, in their personal and professional relationships, and other social settings. Because they can manage their stress levels, they can be more productive, more creative, and more resilient, which can help them to be more effective in their personal and professional lives.

In summary, seeking professional help when necessary can help improve stress management by providing individuals with access to specialized knowledge, skills, and resources that can help them to better understand and manage their stress, which can help them to be more effective in their personal and professional lives.

12. Building and Maintaining a Work-life Balance

Building and maintaining a work-life balance can help improve stress management by helping individuals to prioritize their time and energy, and to ensure that they are not overworking or neglecting other important areas of their life. A work-life balance allows individuals to have time for work, rest, and leisure activities and helps them to manage the demands of their work and personal life more effectively.

For example, an individual who is experiencing stress from work may build and maintain a work-life balance by setting clear boundaries between their work and personal time, and by scheduling regular time for leisure and relaxation activities. They may also prioritize their self-care and make sure to take breaks during their workday, so they can recharge and avoid burnout. Additionally, they may also communicate their needs and boundaries with their employer and colleagues, so they can work together to achieve a work-life balance that works for everyone.

Additionally, building and maintaining a work-life balance can also help individuals to be more effective in the workplace, in their personal and professional relationships, and other social settings. Because they can manage their time, energy, and resources, they can be more productive, more creative, and more resilient, which can help them to be more effective in their personal and professional lives.

In summary, building and maintaining a work-life

balance can help improve stress management by helping individuals to prioritize their time and energy, and to ensure that they are not overworking or neglecting other important areas of their life, which can help them to be more effective in their personal and professional lives.

13. Maintaining Emotional Resilience

Maintaining emotional resilience can help improve stress management by helping individuals to bounce back from difficult situations and to cope with stress healthily and adaptively. Emotional resilience involves developing a set of skills and attitudes, such as flexibility, problem-solving, and a positive outlook, that can help individuals to navigate stress and challenges in their lives. For example, an individual who is experiencing stress may maintain emotional resilience by engaging in activities that promote physical and mental well-being, such as exercise, healthy eating, and getting enough sleep. They may also practice mindfulness, positive thinking, and self-care, and seek social support when needed. Additionally, they may also develop a growth mindset, by seeing challenges as opportunities for personal and professional growth, and learning from their experiences.

Additionally, maintaining emotional resilience can also help individuals to be more effective in the workplace, in their personal and professional relationships, and other social settings. Because they can manage their stress and challenges healthily and adaptively, they can be more productive, more creative, and more resilient, which can help them to be more effective in their personal and professional lives.

In summary, maintaining emotional resilience can help improve stress management by helping individuals to bounce back from difficult situations and to cope with stress healthily and adaptively, which can help them to be more effective in their personal and professional lives.

Health and Wellness

Overview

- ❖ *Significance of Health and Wellness*
- ❖ *The Role of Health and Wellness*
    - ✓ *Maintaining a Healthy Diet*
    - ✓ *Regular Physical Exercise*
    - ✓ *Getting Enough Sleep*
    - ✓ *Managing Stress*
    - ✓ *Building and Maintaining Positive Relationships*
    - ✓ *Cultivating a Positive Mindset*
    - ✓ *Setting and Achieving Personal Goals*
    - ✓ *Building and Maintaining a Work-life Balance*
    - ✓ *Practicing Mindfulness and Relaxation Techniques*
    - ✓ *Seeking Professional help when Necessary*
    - ✓ *Building and Maintaining Emotional Resilience*
    - ✓ *Avoiding Unhealthy Habits*
    - ✓ *Prioritizing Self-care and Regular Check-ups*

SIGNIFICANCE OF HEALTH AND WELLNESS

Health refers to the overall state of an individual's physical, mental, and emotional well-being. Wellness is a broader concept that encompasses not only physical health, but also an individual's overall sense of well-being, including their emotional and mental well-being, and their ability to live a fulfilling life.

The importance of health and wellness can be summarized as follows:

- Physical health: Good physical health is essential for overall well-being and the ability to live a full and active life. It can help to prevent chronic diseases, improve energy levels, and increase lifespan.

- Mental health: Good mental health is essential for overall well-being and the ability to live a fulfilling life. It can help to prevent mental health conditions such as anxiety and depression and improve the ability to cope with stress and adversity.

- Emotional well-being: Positive emotional well-being is essential for overall well-being and the ability to live a fulfilling life. It can help to improve relationships, increase self-esteem, and promote feelings of happiness and contentment.

- Quality of life: Good health and wellness can improve the overall quality of life by increasing the ability to enjoy activities and find satisfaction in life.

- Work performance: Good health and wellness can improve overall work performance and increase productivity.

- Disease prevention: Good health and wellness can help to prevent and manage chronic diseases such as diabetes, heart disease, and cancer.

- Lifestyle management: Good health and wellness can help individuals to lead a healthy lifestyle by making healthy choices and managing stress and emotions.

Examples:

- A person who prioritizes their health and wellness by eating a balanced diet, getting regular exercise, and managing stress, will have a better chance of living a long and healthy life.

- A person who prioritizes their mental and emotional well-being by practicing mindfulness, therapy, and self-care, will have a better chance of living a fulfilling and happy life.

THE ROLE OF HEALTH AND WELLNESS

Health and wellness play a crucial role in achieving success, as they are essential for maintaining the physical and mental energy necessary to perform at one's best. A healthy lifestyle, including regular exercise and a nutritious diet, can improve focus, concentration, and overall productivity. Additionally, a well-rounded wellness routine can help manage stress, which can impact performance and decision-making. Therefore, prioritizing health and wellness can contribute to achieving success in both personal and professional aspects of life. Prioritizing health and wellness can be done by reflecting on the following point:

1. Maintaining a Healthy Diet

Maintaining a healthy diet can help with achieving success in several ways. Eating a balanced diet that includes a variety of fruits, vegetables, whole grains, and lean proteins can help improve energy levels, focus, and overall cognitive function.

Additionally, a healthy diet can help with maintaining a healthy weight and reducing the risk of chronic health conditions, which can improve overall well-being and productivity.

For example, an entrepreneur who starts their day with a healthy breakfast, such as oatmeal with fruit and nuts, may have better energy and focus throughout the morning compared to someone who starts their day with a sugary pastry.

This can help the entrepreneur be more productive and make better decisions throughout the day.

2. Regular Physical Exercise

Regular physical exercise can help with achieving success in several ways. It can improve overall physical and mental health, increase energy levels, and reduce stress. Additionally, regular exercise can help improve focus and cognitive function, which can lead to better decision-making and productivity.

For example, an executive who regularly engages in physical exercise such as jogging or playing sports may be better equipped to handle the physical and mental demands of their job. They may also have better decision-making abilities and be able to solve problems more effectively. Additionally, they may be better able to handle the stress that comes with their job and be more resilient to its negative effects.

3. Getting Enough Sleep

Getting enough sleep can help with achieving success in several ways. Adequate sleep is essential for physical and mental well-being, and it can help improve energy levels, focus, and cognitive function. Additionally, getting enough sleep can help reduce stress, and improve mood and overall productivity. For example, a student who prioritizes getting enough sleep may perform better academically than a student who stays up late studying. This is because sleep is essential for the consolidation of memory, and adequate sleep can improve concentration, attention, and overall cognitive function. Therefore, the student who gets enough sleep will be better able to retain information and perform better on exams. Additionally, the student will be better equipped to handle the stress of school and be more resilient to its negative effects.

4. Managing Stress

Managing stress can help achieve success by allowing individuals to stay focused and motivated, improve decision-making and problem-solving skills, and maintain a positive attitude. Stress management techniques such as meditation, exercise, and time management can also improve physical and mental health, which is essential for maintaining the energy and resilience needed to achieve goals.

For example, a business executive who can manage stress effectively may be able to handle high-pressure situations and make sound decisions that lead to successful business deals. They may also be able to maintain a good work-life balance, which can prevent burnout and improve their overall well-being.

5. Building and Maintaining Positive Relationships

Building and maintaining positive relationships can help achieve success in several ways. Positive relationships can provide emotional support, guidance, and mentorship, which can help individuals navigate challenges and achieve their goals. Strong relationships can also provide access to resources, networks, and opportunities that would otherwise be unavailable.

For example, a young professional who has built positive relationships with colleagues and mentors within their industry may be more likely to be promoted or receive job offers than someone who is more isolated. They may also be able to access valuable information and resources that can help them succeed in their field. Additionally, having a good relationship with team members in a company can lead to a better work environment and teamwork which can lead to better performance and success.

6. *Cultivating a Positive Mindset*

Cultivating a positive mindset can help achieve success by helping individuals to focus on their strengths and resources, rather than their limitations and challenges. A positive mindset can also lead to greater resilience, motivation, and creativity, which can be essential for achieving goals. Additionally, a positive mindset can help individuals to maintain a sense of perspective and optimism, even in the face of setbacks and obstacles.

For example, a businessman with a positive mindset may be more likely to persevere through the difficulties of starting a business, and to come up with innovative solutions to problems. They may also be more likely to attract investors, customers, and talent to their business, as a positive attitude is contagious. Additionally, a student with a positive mindset is more likely to be motivated to study and achieve good grades, and even overcome the challenges that may arise during the learning process.

7. *Setting and Achieving Personal Goals*

Setting and achieving personal goals can help achieve success by providing direction and focus, and by giving individuals a sense of accomplishment and progress. When individuals set clear and challenging goals for themselves, it can help them to stay motivated and engaged, and to make better use of their time and resources. Additionally, achieving personal goals can build self-esteem and confidence, which can be essential for achieving success in other areas of life.

For example, an individual who sets a personal goal to learn a new language may achieve success in various areas of their life such as getting a better job, traveling abroad, and communicating with people from different cultures. This person may also achieve a sense of personal satisfaction and accomplishment from learning a new skill, which can boost their self-confidence and motivation to set and achieve other goals.

Additionally, setting and achieving personal goals can be a driving force for personal growth and self-improvement which are essential for achieving success in the long run.

8. Building and Maintaining a Work-life Balance

Building and maintaining a work-life balance can help achieve success by reducing stress and burnout, increasing productivity and effectiveness, and improving overall well-being. When individuals can balance their work and personal responsibilities, they are more likely to be able to focus and be productive when they are working, and to have the energy and mental clarity to enjoy their personal lives.

Additionally, a work-life balance can help individuals to avoid burnout and maintain a positive attitude, which can be essential for achieving success in the long run.

For example, a business executive who prioritizes a work-life balance may be able to handle high-pressure situations and make sound decisions that lead to successful business deals. They may also be able to maintain a good work-life balance, which can prevent burnout and improve their overall well-being.

Additionally, an individual who has a good work-life balance can be more creative and productive at work, as they will have the energy and mental clarity to tackle new challenges.

Furthermore, having a good balance of work and personal life can help to maintain a positive attitude and a good relationship with family and friends, which can contribute to a more fulfilling life overall.

9. Practicing Mindfulness and Relaxation Techniques

Practicing mindfulness and relaxation techniques can help achieve success by reducing stress and anxiety, improving focus and concentration, and increasing overall well-being.

Mindfulness practices, such as meditation and yoga, can help individuals to become more aware of their thoughts and emotions, and to develop strategies for managing them. Relaxation techniques, such as deep breathing and progressive muscle relaxation, can help to reduce physical tension and to promote feelings of calm and relaxation.

For example, a student who practices mindfulness and relaxation techniques may be able to improve their focus and concentration, which can help them to perform better academically. They may also be able to manage test anxiety and stress, which can improve their overall well-being.

Similarly, an entrepreneur who practices mindfulness and relaxation techniques may be able to maintain a clear and focused mind, which can help them to make better decisions and to manage the high stress that comes with running a business.

Additionally, practicing mindfulness and relaxation techniques can help to improve overall physical and mental health, which can be essential for maintaining the energy and resilience needed to achieve success in the long run.

10. Seeking Professional help when Necessary

Seeking professional help when necessary can help achieve success by providing access to specialized knowledge, expertise, and resources that can help individuals to overcome challenges and achieve their goals. Professional help can come in many forms, such as therapy, coaching, consulting, and mentoring. By working with professionals, individuals can gain new perspectives, learn new skills, and develop new strategies for achieving their goals.

For example, an individual who is struggling with anxiety may seek professional help from a therapist or counselor. Through therapy, they may learn coping mechanisms and techniques to manage their anxiety, which can improve their overall well-being and ability to handle stress. This can help them to perform better in their job or studies and achieve success in their personal life.

Similarly, a business executive who is facing a difficult decision may seek professional help from a business consultant or coach. They may be able to provide expert advice and guidance, which can help the executive to make better decisions and achieve success in their business. Additionally, seeking professional help can provide an individual with a safe and confidential space to work through personal challenges and develop the tools to overcome them.

11. Building and Maintaining Emotional Resilience

Building and maintaining emotional resilience can help individuals achieve success by allowing individuals to bounce back from challenges and setbacks, cope with stress and adversity, and maintain a positive outlook. Emotional resilience is the ability to adapt and cope in the face of stressors and challenges. It involves learning to develop healthy coping mechanisms, being able to manage stress, and being able to maintain perspective in difficult situations.

For example, an individual who has developed emotional resilience may be able to handle the stress of a demanding job or a challenging personal situation and still be able to perform well and achieve their goals. They may also be able to maintain a positive outlook and find meaning and purpose in difficult situations. Additionally, an emotionally resilient person can be more effective in managing their emotions and have more control over their reaction to stressors, which can help them to maintain focus and make better decisions. An example can be a salesperson who has built emotional resilience, they will be able to handle rejection and maintain a positive attitude towards achieving their sales goals.

12. Avoiding Unhealthy Habits

Avoiding unhealthy habits can help achieve success by improving physical and mental health, increasing productivity and effectiveness, and reducing stress and burnout. Unhealthy habits such as smoking, excessive alcohol consumption, poor diet, and lack of physical activity can have negative effects on overall well-being and can impede progress toward achieving goals. By avoiding these habits, individuals can improve their physical and mental health, increase their energy levels, and improve their ability to focus and think clearly.

For example, an individual who avoids unhealthy habits such as smoking and excessive alcohol consumption may be more successful in achieving their fitness goals, such as running a marathon. They will be able to train more effectively and avoid health problems that could impede their progress. Similarly, a professional who avoids unhealthy habits such as procrastination and excessive screen time, maybe more productive and effective in their job and be able to achieve their career goals more quickly. Additionally, avoiding unhealthy habits can also help to reduce stress and anxiety, which can be essential for maintaining a positive attitude and achieving success in the long run.

13. Prioritizing Self-care and Regular Check-ups

Prioritizing self-care and regular check-ups can help achieve success by maintaining physical and mental well-being, preventing illness and injury, and identifying and addressing health concerns early on. Self-care practices such as regular exercise, healthy eating, and adequate sleep can help to improve overall well-being and reduce stress. Regular check-ups with healthcare providers can help to identify and address health concerns early on before they become more serious.

For example, an individual who prioritizes self-care and regular check-ups may be more successful in achieving their fitness goals, such as running a marathon. They will be able to train more effectively and avoid health problems that could impede their progress. Additionally, by prioritizing self-care and regular check-ups, this person may be able to maintain their overall health and well-being, which can help them to achieve success in other areas of their life such as their career, personal life, and even in their education.

Similarly, a business executive who prioritizes self-care and regular check-ups may be able to maintain a good work-life balance and avoid burnout, which can improve their overall well-being and ability to make sound decisions that lead to successful business deals. They may also be able to identify and address health concerns early on, which can prevent them from becoming more serious and impacting their performance and overall well-being.

Setting and Achieving Goals

Overview

- ❖ *Importance of Goals*
- ❖ *What Happens After Achieving Goals?*
- ❖ *Strategies for Achieving Goals*
  - ✓ *Setting Clear and Specific Goals*
  - ✓ *Developing a Plan of Action*
  - ✓ *Breaking down Goals into Smaller, Manageable Tasks*
  - ✓ *Prioritizing and Focusing on the most Important Goals*
  - ✓ *Staying Motivated and Committed*
  - ✓ *Building and Maintaining a Positive Mindset*
  - ✓ *Seeking out Resources and Support*
  - ✓ *Measuring Progress and Adjusting the Plan as Needed*
  - ✓ *Staying Flexible and Open to Change*
  - ✓ *Celebrating Small Successes along the Way*
  - ✓ *Removing Obstacles that might Hinder Progress*
  - ✓ *Staying Accountable and Seeking out Accountability Partners*
  - ✓ *Reflecting on Progress and Learning from Mistakes*

IMPORTANCE OF GOALS

Goal setting is important in life because it provides direction and motivation. Setting and working towards specific, measurable, attainable, relevant, and time-bound (SMART) goals can help individuals clarify their values and priorities, and make progress toward achieving them. Additionally, the process of setting and working towards goals can help to build self-confidence and a sense of accomplishment.

Two examples of goal setting in life:

1. Career: Setting a goal to get a promotion or a raise can help to focus one's efforts on developing the necessary skills and networking to achieve it.

2. Fitness: Setting a goal to run a marathon or lose a certain amount of weight can help to focus on developing a consistent exercise routine and healthy eating habits.

WHAT HAPPENS AFTER ACHIEVING GOALS?

After achieving a goal, it is important to take time to celebrate and acknowledge the accomplishment. This can help to build self-confidence and motivation for tackling future challenges. Reflecting on the goal-setting and achievement process can also provide valuable insights for setting and working towards future goals.

Once a goal is achieved, it's important to re-evaluate and

set new goals. Achieving one goal can lead to new opportunities and possibilities, so it's important to continue to set and work toward new goals to keep growing, learning and improving.

It's also important to remember that goals are not a one-time thing, and achieving a goal is not the end of the journey. It's just a step towards a bigger purpose or a continuous process of self-improvement.

STRATEGIES FOR ACHIEVING GOALS

Several strategies can be used to achieve goals, some of which include:

1. Setting Clear and Specific Goals

Setting clear and specific goals can help achieve success by providing direction and focus, and by giving individuals a sense of accomplishment and progress. By setting clear and specific goals, individuals can identify what they want to achieve, and develop a plan of action for how to achieve it. Clear goals also allow for better tracking of progress and make it easier to adjust plans if needed. Specific goals are more likely to be achieved because they are more measurable and there is a clear understanding of what needs to be done to reach them.

For example, a student who sets a clear and specific goal to improve their grades in a particular subject by the end of the semester can break this goal down into smaller, more manageable goals, such as studying for a certain number of hours per week, attending office hours, or seeking help from a tutor. This student can also establish a clear plan of action and track their progress to see if they are on track to achieving their goal. Additionally, this student may be able to identify what is working and what is not, and adjust their plan as needed to reach their goal.

2. Developing a Plan of Action

Developing a plan of action can help achieve success by providing a roadmap for how to achieve a goal, and by giving individuals a sense of direction and focus. A plan of action helps individuals to break down their goals into smaller, more manageable steps, and to identify the resources, time, and support needed to achieve them. It also provides a structure for tracking progress, making adjustments, and keeping motivated.

For example, an entrepreneur who wants to start a business can develop a plan of action that outlines the steps they need to take to turn their idea into a reality. This might include researching the market, creating a business plan, and seeking funding. By breaking down the goal into smaller, manageable steps, and identifying the resources and support needed, the entrepreneur can stay focused and motivated, and make better use of their time and resources. Additionally, having a plan of action can also help the entrepreneur to identify what is working and what is not, and adjust their plan as needed to reach their goal. It can also help them to identify potential obstacles and plan how to overcome them.

3. *Breaking down Goals into Smaller, Manageable Tasks*

Breaking down goals into smaller, manageable tasks can help achieve success by making goals more achievable, and by providing a sense of direction and focus. When goals are broken down into smaller tasks, it becomes easier to see how to achieve them and to track progress. Additionally, by breaking down goals into smaller tasks, individuals can identify the resources, time, and support needed to achieve them. This can also make it easier to manage time, set priorities, and stay motivated.

For example, an individual who wants to run a marathon can break down the goal into smaller, manageable tasks such as creating a training schedule, setting a training pace, and increasing the distance gradually. By breaking down the goal into smaller tasks, the individual can stay focused and motivated, and make better use of their time and resources. Additionally, by breaking down the goal into smaller tasks, the individual can identify what is working and what is not, and adjust their plan as needed to reach their goal. Furthermore, by breaking down the goal into smaller tasks, the individual can also make the goal less daunting and more achievable, which can make it less intimidating to start working on it.

4. Prioritizing and Focusing on the most Important Goals

Prioritizing and focusing on the most important goals can help achieve success by ensuring that limited time and resources are directed toward the most critical tasks and objectives. When individuals can identify and prioritize the most important goals, they are more likely to stay focused and motivated and make better use of their time and resources.

Additionally, by focusing on the most important goals, individuals can reduce distractions and avoid getting bogged down in less important tasks.

For example, a business executive who prioritizes and focuses on the most important goals, such as increasing revenue and expanding market share, may be more successful in achieving those goals than an executive who is spread too thin and trying to accomplish too many goals at once.

This executive can then prioritize those goals and develop a plan of action to achieve them, while at the same time, ignoring less important tasks that may distract them from achieving the most important goals.

Additionally, by focusing on the most important goals, the executive can also make better use of their time and resources and avoid getting bogged down in less important tasks that may not contribute to the success of the company.

5. *Staying Motivated and Committed*

Staying motivated and committed can help achieve success by providing the drive and determination needed to overcome challenges and achieve goals. When individuals are motivated and committed to a goal, they are more likely to persevere through difficulties, stay focused, and make better use of their time and resources. Additionally, motivation and commitment can help individuals to maintain a positive attitude and to find meaning and purpose in their pursuits.

For example, an individual who wants to lose weight may stay motivated and committed to their goal by setting clear and specific goals, developing a plan of action, breaking down the goal into smaller, manageable tasks, and tracking progress. This person may also find a workout buddy to work out with or join a fitness group to stay motivated and committed to their goal. Additionally, this person may also find a way to make the goal more meaningful and personal to them, for example, wanting to be healthy for their children or running a marathon to support a charity, can be great motivators.

It's important to note that motivation and commitment can wax and wane, and it's normal to experience moments of doubt, discouragement, or apathy. However, by staying motivated and committed, individuals can overcome these moments and continue to work towards their goals.

6. Building and Maintaining a Positive Mindset

Having a positive mindset can help you achieve your goals by making it easier to stay motivated, overcome obstacles, and persevere through difficult times. For example, if you have a positive mindset and believe that you can achieve your goal, you will be more likely to take the necessary steps to make it happen. On the other hand, if you have a negative mindset and doubt your ability to achieve your goal, you may be less likely to put in the effort required to succeed.

One example of how a positive mindset can help achieve a goal is a person who wants to lose weight. If they have a positive mindset, they may be more likely to stick to their diet and exercise plan, even when faced with challenges or setbacks. They may also be more likely to believe in their ability to reach their weight loss goal and be more resilient in the face of obstacles. In contrast, if they have a negative mindset, they may be more likely to give up on their goal and feel defeated by any obstacles they encounter.

7. Seeking out Resources and Support

Seeking out resources and support can help you achieve your goals by providing you with the information, tools, and guidance you need to succeed. For example, if you are trying to start a business, seeking out resources such as books on entrepreneurship, mentorship from successful business owners, or networking opportunities with other entrepreneurs can provide you with valuable knowledge and connections that can help you achieve your goal.

Additionally, seeking out support from friends, family, or a support group can also help achieve your goals. They can provide emotional support, encouragement, and accountability, which can be especially important during difficult times or when you are feeling discouraged.

An example of how seeking out resources and support can help achieve a goal is a person who wants to go back to school. If they seek out resources, such as financial aid, scholarships, and information on their chosen field. They can also seek out support from their family, friends, or a study group, which can provide emotional support and help keep them motivated and on track. They can also seek out mentorship from someone who has completed the program they are interested in, which can provide valuable guidance and advice on how to succeed in their chosen field.

8. *Measuring Progress and Adjusting the Plan as Needed*

Measuring progress and adjusting the plan as needed can help you achieve your goals by allowing you to track your progress, identify areas that need improvement, and make changes to your plan as needed. By regularly measuring progress, you can determine whether or not you are on track to achieve your goal, and make any necessary adjustments to your plan to stay on track.

For example, if you have a goal to lose weight, you would measure your progress by regularly tracking your weight, body measurements, and body fat percentage. If you are not seeing the results you want, you might adjust your plan by increasing the frequency or intensity of your exercise, or by making changes to your diet.

Another example is if you have a business goal, you might measure progress by tracking your sales, customer satisfaction, or profit margin, and adjust your plan by changing your marketing strategy, product offering, or pricing, or by increasing your sales efforts, as needed.

Overall, measuring progress and adjusting the plan as needed can help you achieve your goals by keeping you on track, and ensuring that you are making the most efficient use of your time and resources.

9. Staying Flexible and Open to Change

Staying flexible and open to change can help you achieve your goals by allowing you to adapt to new information and changing circumstances. By being open to new ideas and perspectives, you can take advantage of new opportunities and overcome obstacles that may arise along the way. Additionally, being flexible allows you to adjust your plan or approach as needed, which can help you stay on track and achieve your goals.

For example, if you have a goal to start a business, staying flexible and open to change may mean being willing to pivot your business model or product offering if it's not resonating with customers, or being open to new market opportunities that arise.

Another example is if you have a personal goal such as learning a new skill, staying flexible and open to change may mean being willing to try different methods of learning, or being open to feedback and adjusting your approach as needed to improve.

In summary, staying flexible and open to change can help you achieve your goals by allowing you to adapt to new information and changing circumstances, and by keeping you open to new opportunities and ideas that can help you achieve your goals.

10. Celebrating Small Successes along the Way

Celebrating small successes along the way can help you achieve your goals by providing motivation, building momentum, and maintaining a positive attitude. By recognizing and celebrating small accomplishments, you can keep yourself motivated and engaged in the process of working towards your goal. It can also help you to see progress and stay committed to your goal, by feeling a sense of accomplishment, which can increase self-esteem and self-efficacy.

For example, if you have a goal to save money, you might celebrate small successes along the way by setting short-term savings goals and rewarding yourself when you reach them. For example, if you save $500 in the first month, you might treat yourself to a small reward such as a nice dinner or a concert ticket.

Another example is if you have a fitness goal, you might celebrate small successes along the way by setting short-term fitness goals and rewarding yourself when you reach them. For example, if you reach a personal record in lifting weights or running distance, you might treat yourself to new workout gear or a massage.

In summary, celebrating small successes along the way can help you achieve your goals by providing motivation, building momentum, and maintaining a positive attitude. It also helps you to stay committed to your goal, by feeling a sense of accomplishment, which can increase self-esteem and self-efficacy.

11. Removing Obstacles that might Hinder Progress

Removing obstacles that might hinder progress can help you achieve your goals by making it easier to stay on track and make progress toward your goal. Obstacles can take many forms, such as negative thoughts, lack of resources, or external factors. By identifying and removing these obstacles, you can remove barriers to achieving your goal and make it easier to stay focused and motivated.

For example, if you have a goal to start a business, removing obstacles that might hinder progress might mean cutting ties with negative influences, such as friends or family members who discourage you or distract you from your goal. It might also mean seeking out resources and support, such as a business mentor or networking opportunities, to help you overcome any challenges or obstacles you may encounter.

Another example is if you have a personal goal, such as a weight loss goal, removing obstacles that might hinder progress might mean identifying and addressing any underlying emotional or psychological issues that may be contributing to your weight gain, such as stress, anxiety, or depression. It might also mean seeking out a therapist or counselor to help you develop strategies for managing these issues and staying on track with your weight loss goal.

In summary, removing obstacles that might hinder progress can help you achieve your goals by making it easier to stay on track and make progress toward your goal. It can help you to overcome barriers and make it easier to stay focused and motivated, by addressing any underlying issues that might be preventing you from achieving your goal.

12. Staying Accountable and Seeking out Accountability Partners

Staying accountable and seeking out accountability partners can help you achieve your goals by keeping you focused, motivated, and on track. When you make yourself accountable to someone else, you are more likely to follow through with your commitments and make progress toward your goal. An accountability partner can also help you to stay motivated, by providing encouragement, feedback, and support, and by holding you accountable to your goals.

For example, if you have a goal to start a new workout routine, staying accountable and seeking out an accountability partner can help you to stick to your plan.

You can set a schedule to meet with your accountability partner at the gym, or you can set a schedule to check in with each other and hold each other accountable for sticking to your workout schedule.

Another example is if you have a business goal, you can seek out an accountability partner such as a mentor or a business coach, who can provide guidance, advice, and feedback on your progress.

They can also hold you accountable for taking specific actions, such as networking or making sales calls that are necessary to achieve your goal.

In summary, staying accountable and seeking out accountability partners can help you achieve your goals by keeping you focused, motivated, and on track. It increases the chances of following through with your commitments and making progress toward your goal.

It also helps you stay motivated and encouraged by having someone to share your progress with and having someone hold you accountable for your goals.

13. Reflecting on Progress and Learning from Mistakes

Reflecting on progress and learning from mistakes can help you achieve your goals by allowing you to evaluate your progress, identify areas for improvement, and make necessary adjustments to your plan. Reflecting on progress can help you to see how far you've come, and to identify any patterns or trends that may be affecting your progress. By learning from your mistakes, you can make changes to your approach, and improve your chances of achieving your goal.

For example, if you have a goal to start a business, reflecting on progress and learning from mistakes can help you to evaluate the success of your marketing strategies, identify areas where you need to improve and make necessary adjustments to your business plan.

Another example is if you have a personal goal such as learning a new skill, reflecting on progress and learning from mistakes can help you to evaluate your learning process, identify areas where you need to improve and make necessary adjustments to your learning plan. It can also help you to identify any obstacles or challenges that you may be facing and to develop strategies for overcoming them.

In summary, reflecting on progress and learning from mistakes can help you achieve your goals by allowing you to evaluate your progress, identify areas for improvement, and make necessary adjustments to your plan. It helps you to stay focused, motivated, and on track, by identifying patterns and trends that may be affecting your progress and by learning from your mistakes to improve your chances of achieving your goal.

The End

www.ingramcontent.com/pod-product-compliance
Lightning Source LLC
Chambersburg PA
CBHW052345220526
45465CB00003BA/969